IØ157655

Praise for Asking Anna

"In Seliger's quirky debut, a 20-something who's reluctant to propose to his girlfriend brings her to Seattle to visit old friends before he makes his final decision… . Love him or hate him, Steven weighs his options with a unique and strong voice as he searches for the value of commitment in a hookup culture."

—*Kirkus Reviews*

"*Asking Anna* is fantastic novel and I find some of the negative reviewer's comments quite funny."

—"LakeValleyLLC"

"Above all, the novel isn't sweet, or romantic. It's a warning sign of what the feminist movement has done to both women and men. Women are now sluts who engage in premarital sex, and issue ultimatums to get proposals. Men are now womanizers who struggle with the maturation process. Things would be so much better if women could just keep their legs closed, so men would be forced to give up the 'poon carousel.' In India, this kind of behavior would be outlawed… . I recommend all people below the age of 22 put down this pornographic work, and pick up something wholesome instead."

—Manisha Kaura

"This is surely one of the worst books I have ever read."

—Kathy Lopez

The Hook

For Bess

and

For my students, who have taught me so much, much of it inadvertently

The Hook

A Novel

by J Seliger

PART I

Scott Sole

The blog post that briefly made me a national news item—the kind you might've heard about during a late-night comedian's monologue or an outraged friend's Facebook link—went up in May, mercifully close to the end of the school year but not close enough to save my job. The publicity itself provided extra punishment that went beyond losing my job. It cost me my reputation: every time someone looked for "Scott Sole," they found the stories, their truth or lack thereof irrelevant. Real life was following the fiction I was supposed to be teaching.

I can't trace what happened to a single moment, but if I have to choose one it would be this: I remember standing in front of my junior/senior English class, leading a discussion about how the community's perception of Hester Prynne changes over the course of *The Scarlet Letter*. Maybe she starts a pariah and ends a hero. The community around her evolves because of her autonomy and dignity in the face of unjust collective scrutiny.

It's the kind of point that goes over most students' heads even when it's made explicitly. They were happy to mutter "slut" at any girl perceived to be one by the cruel, exacting standards of high school. Most students can't be reached. In teaching, it's often best to shoot for the three to five students who might be awake and receptive. That's probably too generous. One or two would be a success. Teaching is a game of minor achievements, movement by millimeters, the accretion of detail, especially during difficult class discussions.

"What did Hester do wrong?" I said. "So she did it with Dimmesdale. Should sex be a crime?"

"If you do it with an ugly chick," Sheldon O'Neill ventured. He was the kind of guy teachers don't want starting what was supposed to be a serious discussion.

"We don't know anything real about Hester's appearance. That may not be Hawthorn's point. Go deeper."

"She did it, so she pays," Alice Faulhaber said.

"Is she really paying for the sex?" I said. "Or for something else?"

Stacy Leon's hand went up. She might have been one of the five, though she would help herself if she would stop hanging around Arianna Stephenson, who sat, bored, boinging her curls like they might tell her the answer or grant her wish.

"She's paying because she pissed off the people she lives with. If you make enough people mad, they'll get back at you."

"Even if you're in the right?" I said.

"Yeah. But she shouldn't've done it. With, you know, Dimmesdale."

"Why not?"

"Cause it makes her a skank."

"Having sex with one guy?" It wasn't worth interrogating her over the concept of "skank."

"To them, I mean, yeah."

"What about Dimmesdale?" I said. "Does the same standard apply? Is he a 'skank?' "

"I know the deal," Sheldon said. "You offer *any* guy, even a guy who's a priest—"

"Minister," I corrected. "Priests are usually Catholic."

"Whatever. Pastor. You offer him the chance to hit it, he's gonna hit it. It's that simple. Guys are guys. Players is players wherever they are."

"No," Stacy said. "Not all guys are like that."

"You just don't want to think they're like that."

"My ex-boyfriend isn't."

"How d'you know?"

Stacy stuttered.

The class went, "Oooooooo." Koral Davis exchanged high fives and fist bumps with Sheldon. Things were stumbling out of control—my classrooms rarely spiral out, since "spiral" implies a neat trajectory—and I wanted to get back to the nature of transgression, which Stacy was trying to express without knowing the words.

"Okay, okay" I said. "Sometimes we can understand the end of a work by looking at the beginning. Think about this: where does *The Scarlet Letter* start?"

Many furrowed brows. The more diligent opened their books, a reassuring sign that some students might have read the novel. The less diligent didn't have books to open.

"The jail?" Stacy said.

"Right. This isn't a trick question. The story starts *a*fter the act that starts the plot, so to speak. *The Scarlet Letter* isn't really about what Hester does—or what Dimmesdale does,

I should say, since it takes two to, you know… It's about the consequences, the community's reaction."

Silence. Epiphanic or confused?

"Let's try this," I said. "What do we really know about Hester?"

Silence.

"About her inner life?"

"Nothing?" Stacy said.

"Nothing—why do you say that?"

"We never really get inside her."

"Too bad," Sheldon said. "I bet she's ti—"

"Right, Stacy," I said. "We never know how she feels. Some of you suggested earlier that she is a, uh—" I struggled for a euphemism "—woman of adventurous temperament. How many of you think of yourselves that way?"

Sheldon's hand went up. More laughs. He announced, "I'm a playa, baby."

"How many of you have thought about others that way?" I said. "Or called others… unfortunate names?"

Almost all the hands went up, except for the students who weren't paying any attention. Showing hands forced them to participate by not participating.

Jay Warren—smart, but not as smart as he thought and a bit lazy to boot—walked in to hand me a pink slip. Notes like it were distributed all the time, and the pinks were notorious because they denoted the administration.

I glanced at the writing, looked up, and went back to the note: it wasn't for a student.

"I guess I'm going to the principal's office," I said.

The whole class went, "Oooooooo" again. I laughed. Teachers weren't afraid of the principal because our union was more powerful than any principal. As long as you showed up to work, didn't drink in front of students, and didn't trade sex for grades, you were pretty much immune.

• • •

Stacy Leon

Me, Arianna, and Sheldon were hanging out at Sheldon's dad's. It's this giant loft in Belltown with a funny name. Mosher. Mosler. Whatever. Sheldon had a bedroom made of walls like the ones in offices. Movable, really thin ones. Him and his dad were more like roommates than, you know, father and son.

Sheldon's room mostly had girls printed from the Internet pinned to the wall, and a couple guys in bands. Snake Pit. Seven Mondays. Drake. Being there intimidated me, until I realized the four-foot poster of some chick in a bikini was a fantasy, not a comparison. It was a terrible place to revise our papers, but it was available and Sheldon's dad was almost never home. When his dad wasn't working he was working women. Arianna claimed she wanted to fuck him.

When we got bored in Sheldon's room we went to the kitchen and kinda worked at a long, L-shaped counter, where a bunch of booze bottles were on risers, like they were ready for their class picture. Sheldon's dad let us have a taste pretty much whenever we wanted, and Arianna *wanted*.

Arianna had to be thinking about Scott's class: her parents were going to take her Jetta away if she got below a 2.8 again. Chemistry was already a lost cause. So was pre-calc. In English we could argue grades, and I remember my sister, Melissa, saying that in college people major in English because they can't major in something harder.

I tried to help Arianna, I really did. If I'd helped her more, I don't think she would've gotten herself and Scott and everyone else into the mess thing.

"This stupid paper is going to kill me," Arianna said.

"What's it about?" I said.

"Some girl in the Middle Ages who gets a red letter on her boobs calling her a slut."

"That's what *The Scarlet Letter* is about, not your paper," I said. "I mean, like, the letter calls her a slut? Isn't that impossible?"

"You know what I mean. She's a slut, like Mr. Sole said. I don't care that she had a baby or whatever."

"You should feel for her, girl," Sheldon said. He stopped texting and mimed a pregnant belly. He's always saying stupid, mean stuff. Kind of like his dad, who would stare at me like I was one of his secretaries. Or "Executive Assistants" as he called them.

"Didn't you turn in your first draft a week ago?" I said.

"I forgot to do it," Arianna said. "Mr. Sole gave me an extension."

"Why?"

"I, like, asked for it?"

"That's it?"

"I still have to write the stupid thing."

"He writes a blog, you know," Sheldon said, looking up from his phone. "Mr. Sole."

"Bout what?" I said.

"Books and stuff. Really boring. Like his class."

"Let's see!" Arianna said. Anything to stop writing. She'd already checked Facebook 10,000 times. I'd seen at least five updates, three about how hard it is to write. Melissa sometimes says that writing is the easiest thing in the world because you sit at the computer and do it, but I haven't seen her do any writing since she got out of college.

Sheldon kept at his phone. A game, maybe. He played with himself a lot.

But I wanted to see Scott's blog too. I had a laptop. I think my sister mentioned that he wrote online. This time, though, I searched for Scott Sole on Google. A doctor was the first hit, then a singer, but the third said, "The Sole of Man is Books."

The first post was something about *The Scarlet Letter* and the things we'd talked about in class. You could tell Mr. Sole cared because he spent a lot of time thinking about things he was teaching. Most teachers make you wonder if they use SparkNotes too. One time we were reading *Hamlet* and Mrs. Chandler got caught with SparkNotes, and she sent Jon Karr to Principal Shore's office when he pointed it out.

The next post was about a guy named Dan Ariely, then Cupcake Royale, then Francine Prose's *Blue Angel*, then how to install a hook in drywall. Boring, all of them, I thought, until I scrolled down and saw the picture of the girl.

"Oh my God," I said.

At the same time, Sheldon's dad rolled in with Chinese. Not a Chinese person—Chinese food. He's the kind of guy you could imagine bringing home a massage therapist. Two of them, one for Sheldon. My oldest sister's a massage therapist, but not the happy ending kind. The real kind. At least, I hope so. Melissa was student-teaching at Herbert. Lame. Try going to high school with your angelic sister hovering over you, the one your mom compares you to all the time, and you'll know why I wanted to stay away from home so bad.

Sheldon's dad yelled about dinner. Arianna and Sheldon wanted to eat, but I was still fascinated by the post and what

Scott did on the weekends. And the picture of the girl. He saved it for the very end. He was like that, an eat-your-vegetables kind of teacher. Rewards are worth waiting for. Writing first, then the goodies.

But I gasped when I saw the dirty stuff we were looking at. Where were his morals? I started thinking: What else might we find?

Scott Sole

I write a book blog as a creative outlet. If you were stuck teaching mostly aliterate students for seven hours a day, you'd want a place for art too. I know teachers in bands, teachers who do standup, teachers who make mumblecore. They're the minority. Most teachers go home at night and watch TV or mess around on the Internet, like our students, but the best ones have something else, like the X factor in a great lover.

They're passions we indulge when we're not trying to guide dense 16 year olds into understanding how life in the nineteenth century might have been materially different from our own, but the fundamental sources of drama and conflict remain stable: sex and resource allocation, with a tiny smidgen of intellectual curiosity. Teachers can't say so in class, though, so I say it online.

When I imagine starting graduate school, I see myself using the blog's posts as the basis for articles and an eventual dissertation. But then I imagine who reads academic articles—nobody—and the fantasy withers. Academic articles are verbosely facile. Financial realities intrude too. I've been teaching long enough that I don't want grad-student pay. Payment in pussy is only attractive to guys who haven't earned real money. After five years, I, like most teachers, thought about whether I'd go to thirty on the job and get the retirement package. Real money in teaching is back-loaded. Always follow the money and the DNA. The blog might be the only means I have of self-expression beyond the classroom, where it's hard to have a real conversation. Real conversations get teachers in trouble. Best keep those to friends, or strangers online.

You can connect the post that made Laura Shorewell call me in like a truant student to Kate Everett, the woman I was dating. I'd never met anyone like her. Sure, I'd *read* about women like Kate, but I'd never managed to date one. There were somewhat wild girls in college, but knowing wildness exists is different from seeing a live lion prowling. The difference between a house cat and a wild, coffee-shitting civet isn't just size.

I shouldn't have met Kate when I did. By then Melissa wasn't just back but working under me, so to speak. There was a better-than-even chance she wanted to resume our dalliance, our fling, our hookup, which always had the smell of the whiteboard, dry-erase marker, and textbooks despite beginning and ending in the innocent summers.

But when Melissa began teaching I was straggling out of a failed relationship, and she started the semester with a long-distance boyfriend; by the time he was out Kate was in, in part because it's rarely a good idea to flirt from a position of weakness with a woman who has a boyfriend. One night Melissa made an overture that originated in alcohol and horniness, and that I wanted to accept but didn't. Women are used to being the rejecters, and when they're the reject-ees, it makes them angrier than a cat dunked in a bath, but we still got on okay.

I needed to explore new ways of meeting women: most of them had fallen into my lap through conversations at bars, at coffee, at friends' parties, but the older I got the more I needed to try. So despite Melissa, I left the ad on *The Stranger's* Love Lab because I'd exhausted the dating possibilities presented by friends and friends-of-friends. When college ends, you no longer meet dozens of new, promising girls in the course of everyday life. So you hit the tedious bars if you're into that sort of thing and, like everyone else, the Internet, which makes women as easy to approach as a song.

Kate and I "met" through Love Lab, where I had already met some unexciting girls who only became more exciting with their clothes off. She responded to my initial tease about the guitar in one of her photos, claimed to be 23, liked her eggs poached, didn't smoke cigarettes but would puff a little J, liked *Reservoir Dogs* and *The Notebook*. A dozen other statistical factoids reveal as little about her as jacket copy does about a book. For guys the real questions are simple: could she be cute and does she want to meet with me? (Women want to know: Is he safe? Is he good enough? Should I bother finding out? In the absence of evidence that other attractive women have already vetted him, the latter question is salient.)

We arranged for a drink at Canon, a converted house made into airy bar with bottles of booze stacked like wine behind the counter and tables by some Herman Miller wannabe. She walked in like sex. It wasn't any one thing, but sometimes a girl has that gait and look that says she's into it more than she's into her job or her inane friends or her phone.

The flirting started easy. Kate and I chatted on one level about the bare surfaces of life: occupations, goals, funny stories that implied sexual vigor, both of us promisingly eager to see about our physical chemistry.

Kate rolled into concocting stories based on the people sitting around us, like a novelist: he must be a jockey, meeting his friend's sister. Why the sister? Look at her body language: they've been set up. Or, no, the brother's angry. It's a secret. And so on. Two drinks apiece and I couldn't trust myself to drive if I'd needed to.

Hands found each other's knees and then lower thighs. I didn't know where the evening was going. We debated whether *Cosmo* was good for women and its compatibility with feminism; Kate said no, since *Cosmo* just taught women to be sex objects, and while I agreed, I also argued that it gave women confidence they might otherwise lack—high school and college girls read *Cosmo* because they don't know any better. Popularity exists for reasons, even if the reasons are bad. I'd met plenty of women who hated their bodies, were afraid of getting into bed and worried too much about what they would do once they got there. Kate conceded my point but held her position. "What makes you, Scott, an expert on how women think and feel?"

"What makes *you* an expert?"

"I *am* one."

"Okay, yes, you're a woman. You are therefore you are, but, really—how many have you slept with?"

"Isn't it a bit early to go that deep?"

"It's relevant: I see women when they're at their most insecure and vulnerable. Guys who know what they're doing have to learn to assuage that vulnerability."

"Assuage: nice SAT word."

"If it fits, it fits." I waggled my martini glass suggestively and nonsensically.

We doled out tidbits of immoderate disclosure to see if the other liked to talk about sex. We did, though Kate didn't answer my question about other girls. Not then. Talk sometimes leads to action.

"We should get a drink at my place," I said.

"You drive?"

"Never, with this," I said, holding up the now-empty martini glass. "Safety first. Enhances the pleasure, no?"

"Usually."

"Good. You're up for another?"

"Yeah."

"We'll Uber. Don't worry—I won't behave."

Sheldon

I never liked Mr. Sole because he didn't like me. It's obvious when the teachers don't, and it's totally unfair. They're not supposed to play favorites. It also got to be pretty obvious why Stacy was his favorite and why she got what I should've. I wanted to be an editor. No chance with him discriminating against me because I'm not a girl who can fuck him.

You ask me, he deserved everything he got. The only surprising thing is how long it took.

Sure, Arianna admitted that the stuff she said happened didn't. But who cares? Mr. Sole is the kind of teacher who *would* do that. I'm glad he's never going to stand in front of us again. Not that I care now.

• • •

Stacy Leon

I walked into my own house around 9:00, still dizzy from reading Mr. Sole's sex post. We lived in northern Capitol Hill, south of the U-District, not too far from Arianna's. It was a house my grandparents passed down to my mom, and it looked as little on the outside as it felt on the inside. Neighbors had torn down their 1950s houses and built three-story beasts, with basements sunk into the hill and big windows that let you peer in. Mrs. Dundy, who lived across the street, had sold her house and moved to an old-lady home, and mom said the couple who bought it weren't asking whether they'd tear her place down, but how big the new one should be.

Melissa—my sister, the nerd—was grading journal entries in the common room. She's always grading. Like it matters. Give everyone an A and she wouldn't have to grade. We could be happy.

"Is mine in there?" I asked.

She shook her head like a distracted golden retriever. She'd become less friendly since becoming a teacher. student teacher. Bullshit-teacher.

I dropped next to her on the couch. Melissa shifted away, like I was contagious. She'd gotten fatter since she came home from NYU. Took more space, made a bigger indent in the red leather. I was never going to be like her. I was never going to be fat.

"Guess what I found today?" I said.

"A life?" Melissa said.

"Better. Mr. Sole's blog. You ever read it?"

"Of course. I've edited many of his posts."

"Really? When?"

"Oh, you know."

"Did you edit the one about the hook?"

"What d'you mean?"

I opened my computer to show her.

• • •

Scott Sole

At my apartment I made Aviations: gin, Luxardo maraschino liqueur, lemon, and crème de violette, and a maraschino cherry at the bottom as a reward. I'd made many for Melissa. My hands were surprisingly steady, like they knew the stakes, and I appeared competent in Kate's eyes as I reached into cabinets, measured, poured, squeezed, shook. Women like competence. Competence and power drive the crushes girls develop on their teachers. Kate watched me, maybe to be sure I didn't slip something in. I liked that. Or she liked me, and we like to watch the people we like.

I touched her forearm. She smiled like a green light, the orgastic (or is it orgiastic?) green light Gatsby sees, and I moved into the grab, hold, kiss, coming away smiling. I passed her the Aviation when she was still flush. From the kiss, from hope, from Canon's drinks; alcohol is sex. So is music. Canon's drinks were like candy for adults. My roommate, Ryan, was asleep in the other room; he had to get up early to drive the Purple Coffee Truck in the morning. He liked to listen.

The kiss almost morphed into more, but I backed off. Push-pull: this time it gave Kate time to sip her drink.

Everything about the apartment that was somewhat nice—the black and tan folding bookshelves in the short hall that led to our rooms, the large, dark wood buffet with condoms stashed inside—was mine. Ryan contributed rent and, occasionally, conversation. Nothing was dirty enough to cockblock.

Kate noticed the decor and thought better of me for it. We sat close on the couch like we wanted to get on each other, sipped our drinks, felt the vibe, sex simmering in the living room. Always assume she wants to get on you until proven otherwise. I paid little attention to her words until she asked an essential question.

"Have you had many—adventures—with people from Love Lab?"

"Some," I said. "You?"

"You go first. I asked."

"That how it is?"

"Yeah." Flirty, head down, smiling to her drink.

"Okay. I went out with a girl who was the manager at Pagliacci's Pizza, the one in the U-District. We stayed out too late, and when I asked her what it was like working in a real kitchen, she said she could show me. She did."

"And …?" Kate said.

"And those counters are just about the right height."

"For what?"

"Rolling pizza dough. Making curry. Can you think of anything else?"

"Some things, yes."

"Tell me," I said.

"You don't need me. You're an imaginative boy. Show me."

I did. Casual sex can change your life and be hazardous for your mental well-being. That's the only real explanation I have for what I did. Those who aren't ready to have their lives changed should probably abstain. When I was younger, I worried about life changes, until one day I was a college sophomore and realized, with the power of a Dedalus epiphany, that I was ready for it. Then my real life began, and different women reincarnated me over the years. None like Kate.

After her story I kissed her again. She replied. I stopped, took her glass, and set it on the table next to mine, both still containing a thimble of liquor. She needed the same thing I needed. She held a finger to my lips and reached for the maraschino cherry. When she finished, I kissed her again and maneuvered her on top of me, forcing her knees to either side. She wore a knee-length skirt that rode up. There is nothing sexy about knees until they're spread for more than a squat. We kissed as she rubbed, telling me so much without speaking. Her body pulsed to an unseen rhythm.

"We shouldn't do this," Kate said.

"You're right," I said. "This is so wrong." A line that disarms women. Say what they're thinking before they have a chance to say it.

I reached my hands under her ass, held her, and stood from a seated position. I feared my back would give out. She wrapped her legs around me and let me carry her to the bedroom for all those delightful things you've been erroneously told you shouldn't do on a first date.

Stacy Leon

Melissa was a long time on her computer. Who was she talking to? It was getting late. I texted, mostly Arianna, sometimes Sheldon, and occasionally our other friends, like Bill Wilson. Bill, who I wanted to be my boyfriend but who never would.

People always tell me that I should admire my sister, but I don't. She's so boring. Her idea of a fun Saturday night is reading. Yeah, I'll read too when it's assigned, but I need to get out. Have some fun. When I was in middle school and she was a senior, I'd sneak out of the house while she was editing the newspaper. Was it her fucking job? Was she getting paid for it? Fuck no.

"Since when do you read Scott's blog?" Melissa said, in a tone you'd expect if we'd been watching him shower.

"Since always."

"Why?"

"I like it."

One bad thing about a sister like Melissa is that she can read your mind. I didn't like what she saw.

"Do me a favor," Melissa said. "Don't tell anyone about this. Not until I talk to him. Okay?"

"Um, okay."

"Wait—does Arianna already know?"

"Kinda."

"Who else?"

"Sheldon."

"Then everybody knows. Haven't you learned your lesson about him?"

I shrugged. Melissa asked for Arianna's number. She'd unfriended Arianna on Facebook when she started teaching, too. Must be serious, and she looked like she'd been told Scott was dead.

Arianna didn't pick up like she never did. Melissa left a message, then sent a text. She got up to go to bed.

"Can I use your computer?" I said.

Melissa sighed and logged out of her user account and handed me her Mac. As soon as she left, I switched back. Her password was newyork4eva, like it had been since she was in high school and infatuated with the city instead of a sexy guy like normal girls. Didn't even want to be a model.

I opened Firefox to see what Melissa was looking for.

• • •

Scott Sole

My apartment was still in the U-District, even though I'd outgrown the drunk college occupants and Ave Rats. But it was a straight bus ride south to reach Herbert High, where I taught, and the important parts of Capitol Hill, where I drank, danced, and chased women.

The morning after we met, Kate and I fooled around some in bed, getting started, but she stopped me—*for brunch*. I thought our thing was over until she explained, in that low throaty voice that emerged when she was aroused or looking forward to being aroused, which were much the same thing.

She changed her underwear and shirt, all stashed in her bag—she'd planned or anticipated staying over. We caught a bus south to Crave, which had opened at a new location on 12th, in the ground-level shops of a new set of condos that had windows shaped like half a hexagon, as if telling us that archers might peer out instead of nerds. The restaurant itself was clean and, most importantly, large, with two rooms interrupted by a narrow hallway that had bathrooms and kitchens incongruously placed on one side. Pillars interrupted lines of sight. The sort of place where it was easy to lose track of who was where, when, and why.

Crave was three-quarters full and poorly lit, like a bar. We took a booth along the left side, only a few steps from the narrow passage that led to the bathrooms. As soon as she sat, Kate uncrossed her legs, doing the naughty-student thing. I ran my hand lightly along her thigh, barely tickling, then grabbed it. Like a pro, she gave little outward sign other than the quickening of her breathing like an athlete warming up. I felt it too: we were doing something crazy, dangerous, a feeling I hadn't really felt since Melissa, and before her since sneaking out of my own house in middle school. What they say is true: the forbidden is extra hot. No wonder so many teachers have these problems. Too few taboos left to violate.

With a free hand Kate pushed her silky brown hair off her neck, offering me a long pale expanse to quickly run my tongue.

Our waiter appeared with just enough warning for us to unruffle. We ordered, water for me and coffee for Kate, and took a cursory look at the menu, with its sensuously curly letters, though we weren't there for what everyone else was there for. Bad art stared at us from the walls, with prices in the low hundreds of dollars. I picked huevos rancheros with the salsa verde at random. Kate deliberated. She struck me as the kind of person who would try a dozen flavors in a gelato shop when the real goal was to get home and naked, as the kind of person who would use delay as foreplay.

Kate asked: what did the waiter think of the potatoes? Was the vegetable hash really as hearty as the corned beef? If the French Toast was so thick, how did they ensure the center cooked? What did she think about no-carb lifestyles? I wanted her to get on with it until I realized she was heightening the pleasure through the normalcy of the conversation. She liked that I kept my eyes on her. Did the waiter know something was up? Did everyone?

The waiter left. I began touching Kate again, and she slid a hand underneath her skirt to guide me. She wore a thong. Most of them do when they expect action, although the inverse isn't true: wearing a thong doesn't automatically show they want action.

I'd not done these kinds of things in public, except maybe for fooling around in the library when I was a college student. This had more frisson. Consequence. Life felt more consequential.

I was in an erotic fog when the waiter appeared to proffer more coffee and almost caught me with my hand in the cookie jar. Kate took a refill and when the waiter departed said she needed to go and promised to be only a minute. I watched the swish of her black-skirted rear as she made her way to the bathroom. Waiting was hard, in more than the obvious manner. She came back.

"Almost forgot—these are for you," she said, passing me her underwear. Adore Me, not Victoria's Secret. An Internet-smart girl. The underwear confirmed that Kate was enjoying the adventure, and it went in my pocket like a fortune. I whispered to her that I was going to go to the bathroom and she should come about a minute after, tap twice on the door, wait, and tap a third time.

"Your face is red," Kate said. "Too warm in here?"

"Absolutely," I said.

The bathroom was faux homey, with a rounded sink on the wall and more bad art, but this time of a gushing river, as if to put the occupant in the right frame of mind. I unzipped, prepped, put a condom on. The taps came. Kate was in.

As soon as the door latched I was mashing Kate into the wall. We tried standing, but the position was too awkward. We tried standing but with me holding her by her ass until I grew tired. So I pushed her over the sink, thinking about how she'd said she wanted a guy who was passionate, who was willing to try new things, who understood that not all wants can be communicated verbally: someone who wasn't like the Amazon programmers she kept finding, who were nerdy and weak or else algorithmically dominant, like they'd read in a book that women like to be held down. For most people words don't create attraction. The body does.

We didn't speak with words. Kate used one hand to balance herself and a second against the mirror, with her skirt hitched around her waist. I used my right hand to stroke her and the left to hold her neck. It didn't last long, by intent for once, and when I said, "I'm going to—" it was already too late. Based on the way Kate arched her back and squeezed, she knew too.

As soon as I pulled out, she faced me.

"I want to finish," she said.

"I want you to too," I said. "Almost as much as that, I don't want to get caught. Do you?"

"No. Yes. Maybe."

"That stupid teaching-license thing. How close?"

She gave an obstinate, cute little jump in frustration. Someone knocked. Kate reached an arm around my neck to draw me close and whisper, "When we get home."

"Practice in the booth?" I said.

"Under the table?" she asked. She smiled, flirty. "I don't think I can, not in public without being totally obvious."

Kate checked herself in the mirror; she wasn't too mussed. Someone not seeking signs wouldn't notice. She straightened, kissed me, and unlocked the door to stride purposefully out, a practiced-seeming maneuver. She could've been a young executive or lawyer.

I relocked the door, feeling so alive, so full of wonder, like I rarely had before. Ecstatic experience is underrated.

Someone jiggled the knob again. I conspicuously washed my hands and called, "Just a minute."

When I came out I couldn't help smiling. A server was exiting a batwing door to my right. To my left, where I needed to go to get back to our table, I was momentarily flummoxed by a woman with her arms crossed under her breasts. The problem was that I recognized her. The problem deepened because the context was all wrong: Arianna, a student, waited for the bathroom. She was a face from school. Maybe she didn't know what we were doing. No—I wanted to believe she *couldn't* have known.

"Hi, Arianna," I said.

"Hi, Mr. Sole," she said.

I refocused over her shoulder. Stacy Leon and a guy—Jaime?—were sitting there. Worse, so was Melissa Leon.

Melissa Leon

Stacy is my little sister, and she's as obnoxious as only little sisters can be. Arianna complemented her that way, but with a bitchy edge. Because of an unfortunate event involving salacious texts and video sent to a sleazy guy named Sheldon, she's Stacy's only somewhat-real friend. Girls are awful to each other at that age. Sheldon seemed then like the kind of person who'd go to a *Lusty Lady* peepshow and make lewd offers to the dancers, or perhaps end up managing a club in Portland. Maybe he had something in common with Scott. I haven't seen Sheldon in so long that I can't say what he's like now, but the older I get the more I realize that boys don't mature: they only get older.

That morning in Crave I felt the familiar pit, jealousy, form in my stomach when I saw the girl Scott was with. My only consolation was that I was prettier. Much prettier, even if I didn't look it in jeans from yesterday and a Gore-Tex raincoat. The girl wore a skirt that must've made her ass freeze popsicle hard. It was cold and wet outside, but here she was, prancing around like some of the girls I knew at NYU who thought every street was a catwalk. That Scott was with her showed that he wasn't so different from the rest of them, in a way I found infuriating and, though I didn't want to admit it, arousing.

I'd admired Scott. The first year he taught at Herbert, I was a senior and the newspaper editor. I showed him the novel I wanted to write—about a beautiful but misunderstood girl with a fabulous crush on a distant, older man with a mysterious past and wounds inflicted by a cruel mistress, who she eventually coaxes into loving again. He corrected my grammar, suggested further reading, and didn't crush my dreams. Instead he warned me that the only valid reason for writing a novel is because the writer feels she must, or go mad, or die. A literary crush was not among the items on his approved list of writerly inspirations. I didn't care.

Later, he taught me more about life than about commas. Now that I was in Seattle, doing my student teaching, I kept expecting to go back to the way we were, but he'd had an outbreak of ethics that I kept expecting to clear up.

That morning I was at breakfast, thinking about how happy I was not to be a high school student, when Arianna came back breathless. I saw why: Scott was hovering near the bathroom, watching me, waiting for me to look at him. I waved, sort of, not real sure about what to do.

"It's the weirdest thing," Arianna said. "I was waiting in line for the bathroom and the chick he's with came out."

"So what?" I said.

"I tried to go in, but the door was still locked. I asked the hostess if something was wrong with the bathroom door, and she looked at me funny, when Scott came out. How'd he get in?"

"Oooohhh," Stacy said. "They went in *together*."

"Unlikely," I said.

"Why?"

"He's a teacher," I said, knowing how little that meant. Seemingly every pothead I've met went into teaching.

"Yeah?" Like Arianna was fucking dying to tell. "You don't know what we saw last week."

Scott Sole

Had I mentioned in class how much I liked Crave for breakfast? Could I have mentioned it at Herbert High's Salsa Club, where I was an advisor and would say things I wouldn't in class? Telling the truth about things that matter is dangerous. Were Arianna and Stacy following me? Seattle wasn't so small a town that we should keep ending up in the same place at the same time. I didn't want to be stalked by two would-be journalists, each pinheaded in her own unique way.

I ate too fast because I was nervous. Kate ate too fast and at most only half her meal because she was horny. She wanted to know about the girls at the table. I sketched Arianna and Stacy, the dumb and the bright bound together by circumstance and choice.

"Where do you know the other one from?" Kate whispered.

"Used to be a student. Her name's Melissa. Now she's a student teacher."

"Boys are going to loooooove being in her class. I don't know if they're going to learn any geometry, or whatever."

"English, yeah. She's very good, though. Pretty doesn't automatically mean stupid."

"Good. Sounds like my type."

"Mine too."

Kate leaned in as if to kiss me. I held off. Enough semi-public displays of affection.

"Did you ever—" Kate said, leaving the question in the air.

"With Melissa? What makes you ask?"

"You don't want to talk about her."

"I'm going to talk *to* her in a minute, once we walk out."

"Will this be awkward?" Kate said.

"For Melissa more than for me."

"I've an idea."

Kate slipped me a note on a napkin: "You mind if I ask her to hang out with us tonight?"

I wanted to say no but didn't want to be the guy who isn't as kinky as the girl, which is one fast way friends-with-benefits and relationships die.

"You do the asking," I said. "And don't expect much."

Melissa reacted funny. She knew something was up, beyond the morning-after brunch. She was sensing, maybe, her window of opportunity dwindling. I was annoyed with myself for being too focused, and by that I mean horny, to pay attention to my surroundings. A hazard and pleasure of being human.

On the way out we stopped to say hi and make vague introductions that let Kate's relationship to me remain ambiguous. What could I call her? A hookup? A fuck buddy? I asked Melissa how her weekend was going.

JAKE SELIGER

She said, "I didn't do anything last night. It's like I was a high school freshman again."

"It's astounding," Arianna said.

"Time is fleeting," Stacy said. I wanted to suspend both of them, right there.

"You?" Melissa said.

"I was just hanging out last night," I said.

"Not like last weekend?" Arianna said.

"Less dress up, more sat-is-fact-ion?" Stacy said.

"What do you mean?" Melissa said.

"They saw me at the movies," I said too quickly. "Melissa, how's your *Scarlet Letter* lesson plan?"

Arianna made a gagging motion, like she was going to vomit; I ignored her. Selective attention is a valuable asset.

"Good, good," Melissa said, and she swatted Arianna lightly. Arianna wasn't really paying attention. Stacy was.

"We should go," I said.

Kate almost fell over herself to say to Melissa, "I feel like we haven't gotten to talk."

"Sorry," Melissa said.

"We should all hang out."

"I'd—like that." An answer straight out of male fantasy land. What was going on?

"Tonight? Drinks?"

"How about Canon?" I said.

• • •

Stacy Leon

I said, "Don't you think he was acting weird?"

"If you knew him better," Melissa said, "you'd think that was pretty damn normal. Pretty damn normal. Typical fucking Scott."

She still wouldn't let me order a drink. Bitch. We pressed her for details like English teachers do to us. She'd only shake her head and chug the mimosa she ordered after Mr. Sole left.

Scott Sole

Much later I saw Kate's apartment, which was puzzled in one of the old, bizarrely laid out complexes in Capitol Hill, with pool-table-green carpet in the common areas and a nominal sense of history that was supposed to make up for dilapidation. Knowing what and who was coming, I would've been content in a cardboard box.

In Kate's apartment, bags were everywhere, whether grocery, messenger, purse, makeup, or back. Clothes in much the same way, like the girls whose rooms are inevitably messy in amateur porn. Empty cans in the kitchen. A few on her common-room table.

Not many books, though to her credit there were some, outnumbered by DVDs—and who bothered with DVDs anymore? Some European art films, or, more accurately, highbrow pornography of the sort I aspired to like and make. *Blue is the Warmest Color*, that sort of thing, glorious and notorious among a certain set. She apologized for the mess but obviously didn't care: her interests were elsewhere, in a rich erotic life I hoped to share. Her domestic life, I could do without.

The most vital part of her apartment was the bed, maybe by Casper because she seemed the type, which was clear of debris, large—maybe even a king—and had some attachments poking out the top and sides for tying one up. I meant to grab her, throw her on it and forcibly go down on her, but I was transfixed by a large hook on the wall. It sat on a long, vertical track, allowing it to be adjusted to different heights depending on the person affixed to the sex toy. Kate was about 5'6" and the hook about 6', or another couple inches above my eye level. She'd have to stretch on her tiptoes to reach.

"You like that?" Kate said.

"What's it for?"

"Think about it—you're a smart boy."

She came over, languidly, lifting her hands above her head as if they'd been handcuffed. The chain would be secured by the hook. She would be deliciously vulnerable. For the right person.

"I see."

"It's supposed to give you ideas," Kate said.

"It does. Many."

"Girls with submissive tendencies don't like to give directions," Kate said, "but if you use it right, it makes your mind float away into nothing. Not any guy can do it right."

"I've never met a test I didn't ace, aside from an Introduction to Quantum Theory test in college before I wimped out of science, but I should let my actions speak."

"Yes."

"You seemed so quiet the first night we met," I said.

"And now?"

"You seem quiet, but with a certain intensity in your eyes. Complicated. You ever heard of *Never the Face*, by Ariel Sands? A book? Too bad—"

"Scott, please stop talking."

"As I said, you should read it. Anyway, now you seem much more like someone who knows what she wants."

"And is getting it, when you... stop talking."

"For girls... well, it's not that easy to get what you want, I thought, cause whatever label you've been told to use is easier to use than it is to analyze what's really going on, how you really feel. Hell if you know what you really feel. Clarity of purpose is rare. Everyone uses plagiarized emotional rhetoric when we can't figure out what we really feel."

"The only way to get what we want," Kate said, "is to demand it."

"Once we're willing to admit it to ourselves. I like what you're saying. You'd be a good teacher, you know, if you wanted to get out of the nonprofit world."

She laughed. "I don't think so. Not enough patience. And while I don't usually go for younger guys... I'd be tempted. Look at—"

"I know what you mean."

It was like I'd dropped a toaster in her bathtub from the way Kate buzzed and said, "Really? Tell me."

"Don't worry. I've never acted on it. *Really* acted on it, I mean."

"Too bad. We should play student and—" She raised her eyes to the hook.

"We should. Get the handcuffs."

An hour later we were showered and dressed. I was still thinking about the hook.

"How do you put up one of these guys?" I said, giving a quick yank to test stability. The hook didn't move. Not that I expected it to: if it holds a girl thrashing, it'll hold a tug.

"It's not hard. Couple of mollies—the hardware kind, not the drug kind—for the slider-track thing. Got instructions on the Internet."

"Mind if I use your computer? I promise it's not for porn—this time."

Kate paused long enough to show discomfort and said, "Go for it."

Her laptop perched on a desk as cluttered as the rest of the place, but I searched for various combinations on hook installation. Almost all concerned ways to put up plants and pot racks; none dealt with women. A few were about API calls.

"Any luck?" Kate said.

"Not really. You don't remember anything else?"

"No," she said, thoughtful, like maybe she would. "I bet I can reconstruct it. You should write a how-to. I meant to, but I'm not much of a writer."

"Are you suggesting I commence some home improvement projects?"

"Wouldn't be a bad idea."

Arianna Stephenson

That morning at Crave I thought Scott was acting really weird. I kept giggling with Stacy and texting. Melissa tried to grab our phones but she was slow. So slow. No more edge. At brunch she wasn't a teacher and couldn't fucking tell me what to do.

I wrapped my hands across my body and turned my back to Melissa, so it looked like someone was making out with me.

"Oh, Scottie," I said. "You're so good. I love it when you give me an 'A.' Right there, baby, I love your A."

"That's not how she sounds," Stacy said. "It's more like this." She gave a series of short moans, each one cut off like by an inhalation of breath.

"You've both reverted to being twelve," Melissa said. "I have a real job, and I'm done babysitting. You promised—"

"Oh baby," I said. "Yes, with your ruler. All twelve inches."

Melissa sighed. I mean, like, when did she forget how to laugh? I wished Sheldon was with us. He'd laugh. He'd probably try to make out with Melissa too, the manslut.

"Wait," Stacy said, suddenly serious. "Have you ever hooked up with Scott?"

"He's my mentor. He's—" Melissa said.

"Mmmmm," Stacy said. "Sweet teacher-on-teacher love."

"I think he's cute," I said. "I would, you know, that."

"Hottie," Stacy said. "For an old guy."

"He's, I don't know, 28?" Melissa said. "Hardly old."

"He looks surprisingly good in fishnets too," Stacy said, "Considering, you know, fishnets."

"Where'd you see him in fishnets?" Melissa said, sharp this time.

"You don't know?" Stacy said. She turned to me. "She doesn't know."

"She doesn't know!" I said.

Melissa grabbed both of our forearms, rattling plates on the way. The table wasn't too sturdy. They should get new ones. I don't know why Scott liked this place. It was pretty ghetto. No matter what I said I didn't know why Melissa liked that perv Mr. Sole, like *she* was in high school.

"Tell me what you saw," Melissa said.

• • •

Stacy Leon

About a week before the Crave brunch, Arianna and me were hanging out with Sheldon on Saturday night, bored. His dad had disappeared into the city with some busted 25-year-old stripper-type. If my mom knew about Sheldon's family or that he was filming that one time, I'd never get to come over on my own. I wish I could find a less-gross guy to hang out with.

We were wondering what to do, all three of us lined up on the couch with a foot between, texting or chatting with whoever we could think of. I actually didn't know who to call, so I Facebooked and surfed gossip sites, pretending to type now and then. When Arianna and I were younger we'd tortured strange men on video chat but I didn't think that was so smart anymore. She was always the leader but I'd stopped being the follower. Did she still do it alone, showing those men *almost* everything they wanted?

You'd think we were almost normal, except for the reporter's notebook in my purse. Arianna never carried one, even though she wanted to get in the newspaper.

"You ever seen," Sheldon said, "*The Rocky Horror Picture Show?*"

"What's that?" I said.

"Showing at midnight at the Egyptian. I can't explain it—you have to experience it. Like anal." He made a vile gesture.

"Ew," Arianna said. "Isn't it for perverts? The movie, I mean?"

"So you're interested," Sheldon said.

Two hours later we were at the Egyptian, an old brick theater on Capitol Hill that reminded me of an ancient school where kids would get whipped for fighting. Arianna and Sheldon had become freaks for the show. Sheldon wore gold lamé shorts, white tennis shoes laced like he was ready for a game, and a shooter-guy trenchcoat he planned to shed inside.

We met two guys Sheldon knew—Sheldon is five of my six degrees of separation—one short and ratlike, with a wavering mustache that wouldn't help him any, and the other slightly taller and round. He'd never been in the gym. Zero boyfriend material. Plus this girl, Justine, a gothy chick in black, but she was really thin and pretty and had a nice chest.

Sheldon stared at it like he'd find eternity nestled between her boobs. I wish mine were that nice. My mom says I shouldn't compare myself to other girls because I'll give myself an eating disorder, but what am I supposed to do when my best guy friend goes gaga over every girl but me? He sees me like someone who'll always be there if he wants a taste.

Arianna was in this red outfit like a sequin-covered swimsuit: glaze on a donut. I was starting to regret not dressing up. Jeans and a T-shirt made me the freak who stood out. It'd be nice if everyone who was one in real life wore a sign like, "I'm a freak!"

We bought tickets and stood in line. The bigger guy—maybe cute? Two-beers cute?—talked about how he used to play foosball in middle school and now prefers pool. Why was I there. Wasn't there a party somewhere? The guys who were jerks to us at school still like to see us at parties. The guys think we'll be easy. Arianna doesn't prove them wrong. Everyone knows.

Before the movie, there was this Rocky Horror "virgins" ceremony. I refused to go up. Arianna did and kissed some boy, then said she wasn't 18 yet, and the guy running it told her it never happened. She said she often used that method, and he mock-silenced her. The thin rat-guy on my right let his hand drift towards my life, forcing me further and further to the left, next to the gothy girl who whispered with Sheldon.

The movie started, and it was okay until the transvestite showed up. The weirdest part may not have been the on-screen action, but how a bunch of guys dressed as him all pranced on stage. One ran shrieking down the aisle, and, through the makeup, lip liner, and black vest with no shirt underneath, I had a feeling I recognized him. I leaned over the thin guy—let my boob brush against him if that would make him happy—and said, "Arianna!"

I pointed. She didn't get it, until she said, "Really?"

Really. It was Mr. Sole, by how he danced and ran. He was a—much more controlled Rocky. But feral. Damn. Best of both. People shouted at the screen, like they were crazy. No, they *were* crazy. The Rockies went up, Sheldon among them, to chase the transvestites around the theater. When Sheldon came back, laughing, he went, "Yeah! That's him! Uhn!"

The movie made no sense. I'd have to be high to like it. I wished I was high, because Mr. Sole saw us. Scary.

Arianna wanted to make a quick getaway in the lobby, but Sheldon and his girl toy wouldn't let us. Asshole. They stationed themselves near our exit—and Mr. Sole's exit—which left him and his group time to practically walk right into us. Some of them were women dressed in their underwear. Show some self-respect, but I was dying too to know: what makes a grown man wear makeup and dress in drag, especially one who was usually trying hard to be masculine? What, besides the pressure of his friends?

"Girls!" Scott said. "And Sheldon. Have you heard of, 'Don't ask, don't tell?'"

"Uh, kinda," Arianna said. A guy in a man-thong and vest ran by.

"Good. Because that's the principle we want to apply right here, right now."

"What?" I said.

"I don't ask why you're here, you don't tell me. Neither of us tells anyone. Sound good?"

"We should pinky swear," Sheldon said.

"You are such an idiot," Arianna said.

"That means so much coming from you."

"Don't pick on each other," Scott said. "Under pain of detention. You're all … friends."

The joke fell like a cantaloupe off the Space Needle. It was hard to think with Mr. Sole's package on display and his friends making silent fun of us. Sheldon picked things up.

"Mr. Sole, you lookin' good," Sheldon said. "Pretty swole. You been working out? I mean, no homo."

"Uh, no comment," he said. "Look, we should be going." He gestured vaguely to his amused friends. One, a guy, leered at me and said, "You look like your sister. Melissa, right?"

"My sister?" I said. "How d'you know her?"

"Ryan, shut up," said Mr. Sole. "We're out of here. Have a good night."

"Where you going?" Sheldon said.

"Bars. Where else? We're adults. I'd invite you if I could. But, you know …"

"I got a fake."

"I don't know that," Mr. Sole said.

"Let's get a picture," Sheldon said.

"No!" Mr. Sole said, and grabbed Sheldon's wrist before he could pull up his phone. "Don't ask, don't tell, nothing on Facebook, nothing anywhere on the Internet. Silence is golden. No kids and no STIs? Never happened, then. Gotta run. Be safe."

"Peace out, then," Sheldon said, like he was our leader. Confused leader. What Mr. Sole said confused him, but guys still swagger. If they didn't take the lead sometimes, I guess we'd all be standing around with nothing to say. I still wanted to know: how did that guy know my sister's name?

The girl, Justine, turned to me and said, "Was that really your teacher?"

Arianna Stephenson

I told Stacy she *had* to tell Melissa about Scott at *Rocky Horror*. I didn't really know why. I tell everyone everything. People want to know. If I was Melissa I'd want to know.

Stacy Leon

When we finished telling the *Rocky Horror* story at brunch, which was full of interruptions and half finished thoughts and wasn't even *that* much of a story, I was like, what's up with Melissa? I mean, it's not like he went gay-for-pay though you could imagine him doing that kind of thing. Post-breakfast Melissa had gone from her usual talky-but-now-I'm-an-authority-figure self into being not angry exactly but twitchy, like the guy she liked was going to Homecoming with someone else.

Arianna was like, "It was very rude of him not to introduce us to his friends," but I sort of got why.

No, Melissa wasn't unhappy: she was tired. She'd never worked a real job and thought everything was all about being a lifeguard and hooking up and my being my parents' favorite even when she's being a bitch. She'd been sleeping practically all weekend, and not with anyone. She's happier when she's getting it regular and she's not around so much. Part of me wishes she hadn't come back to do her student-teaching thing because our relationship was better when we *weren't* sharing space.

"You okay?" I said.

"What?" Melissa said.

"English, do you speak it? Are. You. Okay? You look lost in space. Or, like, sick."

"Yeah. Sorry. I was just—thinking."

"'bout?"

"Nothing."

Liar. How can you think about nothing? It was so romantic and so sick. She wanted Mr. Sole, all of him, and she knew because of that girl at brunch she'd never get him.

Melissa Leon

I hate competition over guys. It started in sixth grade and never let up. I hate it, hate it, hate it. There're so few guys worth really, really wanting. They're inevitably mobbed with girls. Sheldon isn't even good and yet look at what sick shit he got my sister and Arianna to do. *I* didn't start group sex till college.

Still, if they knew about Scott, my sister and Arianna would be sick too. Or worse, competitive. Stacy might be ready. I'd found by accident unsavory websites on her computer. I knew she'd had a vibrator for years, because I found it on the bathroom counter a week before I left for college. Always a vibrator never a boyfriend: talk about challenge.

Stacy Leon

That *Rocky Horror* sighting of Mr. Sole's bouncing jangling bojangling junk brought us to telling Melissa about Mr. Sole's post. After a minute of sitting there, Melissa got up with new purpose. Like she'd been goosed.

"Done thinking?" I said.

"Yeah," Melissa said.

"So what're you thinking now?"

"None of your business."

"You have a cruuuuu—" I started to say, elongating the syllables like Mr. Sole said poets and singers do.

"Know what? I'll meet up with Scott tonight. I will. It's been…"

"Been what?" I said.

She didn't reply.

Scott Sole

Seeing the three of us at Canon, you'd think we were just friends out having a good time. You wouldn't detect the tension, rippling through the talk of jobs and teaching and how to make it in this economy. Then the tension shifted, as we sought a third opinion about whether *Cosmo* could be an effective means for women to build confidence in bed or merely a tool to make women feel bad. Men or women who feel bad should fix it by squatting and deadlifting rather than buying stuff, but mine is a minority opinion, and on *Cosmo* I came down more on the empowerment side. Kate argued the alternative. Our judge, Melissa, was serenely neutral, like she held the scales of justice, blindfolded. To me *Cosmo* was missing evolutionary biology.

I wanted to wait and simultaneously, impossibly, to skip to the good parts. Porn consists of one-dimensional lives that don't have all the annoying details that make up character included. As we talked the details of the conversation itself blurred. Melissa kept leaning forward, kept touching me. She wanted what she wanted. Like we all do.

Kate Everett

At Canon Melissa was animated in a way that might have been a little bit fake, like Disneyland Paris. But she was still sexy. Wrapped in a blue dress and tights. I don't get crushes on that many girls but this one had an X factor. From what Scott had said I bet she had wild stories about New York. She reminded me of myself: intense, literate, unhappy because of the environment she hadn't made. High school was made brutal for me by girls, for girls. Girl who would've liked to get some but didn't were the worst. Not many girls had figured out how to be who they are without letting the opinions of others affect them. They'll have a good makeout with another girl but deny it in the morning.

When Scott went to the men's, I whispered to Melissa, "Tell me about the first time you kissed a girl."

"Really kissed her?"

"Yeah."

"I was in eighth grade."

"Who was the aggressor?"

"I'm not sure," Melissa said. "Neither of us, really. It just sort of … happened."

"Which means it never happened again."

"How'd you know?"

"I can tell."

"Were you the aggressor with yours?" Melissa said. Without waiting for an answer: "You remind me of Scott in some ways."

"We've spent a little time together—sometimes you meet someone who gets you, and everything clicks. I live for that click."

"Like I was saying," Melissa said, no longer happy with me, "the thing with the girl happened once. We were never the same, around each other. At the time it was novel …"

"Exciting?"

"Yes, but scary."

I put my hand over hers, holding my drink up with the other. "I know," I said.

What was Scott doing in the bathroom? Not like the boy to disappear. Or was it?

"This could be the part where you ask me about hookups with other girls," I said.

"Tell me about your experiences with other women."

She sounded like a reporter. Scott reappeared as I was saying, "I remember one woman who had great taste in shoes and wore these delightful purple Louboutin pumps that were still comfortable to walk in. A lot of her lingerie came in purple because of the shoes. She was hippy, so her pants always stretched a little in front—"

"Great description," Scott said. "Melissa has novelistic tendencies too, you know. Watch out: she might twist your words, or steal from you."

"I like fashion more than fiction," Melissa said. Funny that she went with Scott—he'd wear white sneakers with black jeans, or a dressy coat with a V-neck blue T-shirt. I like a man who dresses nicely. But I liked the promise of what would be next more.

Scott Sole

Did Melissa even *like* Kate? The conversation moved to college stories. Kate spoke of dabbling in girl hookups as a freshman at UW. A guy next to us, wearing a suit, perked up when he overheard, causing Kate to scoot her backless chair closer.

Emboldened by booze, Melissa shared aggressively implausible stories about her experience. She also kept ordering drinks. The second made sense. The third made her loopy. The fourth I finished because she was, simply, drunk, and drunk like I'd never seen her. Canon makes major drinks; two were enough to knock me off equilibrium.

Melissa tried to order a fifth, and I suggested my apartment instead, and she slurred that she thought it an excellent idea. Her words were more like, "s'excellent idea." She stood up wobbly and put out a hand to steady herself on me. The others in the bar stared, at this hot girl who was going to be getting some. I paid the bill. I always do.

Kate smiled at me and whispered, "She's nervous."

"Are you?" I said, loudly enough for Melissa to hear.

"A little," Kate said. "That's the way I like it." Which explained her penchant for Internet dating, which entailed both nerves and the absence of cockblock friends.

Kate tried to keep Melissa from singing in the Uber. Singing is still the stuff of life. At the apartment everything was beside the point. Melissa's reckless mood affected me. Infected me. I liked and didn't like it at the same time. Kate, who probably viewed me as little more than a random guy who could maybe give her what she wanted, made heroic efforts at normalcy and reassuring Melissa. They held hands. They put arms around each other, like they were playing bit parts from *Entourage*, living the fantasy.

Ryan came in while Melissa and Kate were kissing. He goggled. I would've too, if I were him, but I waved him into his room. The damn guy still hadn't gotten back into things after his divorce. I needed a better roommate; this one was just a check.

Melissa didn't notice until after he'd taken off his shoes, then she jumped away, like a parent had caught her 13-year-old self. She mumbled apologies. If she'd been soberer, the gears would've turned: who else could Ryan tell? Girls are always worried, and guys who really know what they're doing know that silence is their ally. Ryan left, but not without taking a great visual gulp of what was on display. Put a burger in front of a starving man and you can't expect him not to salivate. Ryan, however, was impervious to the improving literature, like *The Game*, that I slipped him.

In another circumstance Ryan might've killed the moment. But once he settled in his room, Kate kept up the seduction. So did I. Melissa played the seduced. Most women needed to be chased.

When I unhooked Melissa's bra, I stumbled like *I'd* reverted to 13. But I managed and then was managing Melissa's neck, kissing along it, while Kate worked her front. I suggested we move to the bedroom and carried Melissa to it, and in it I undid Kate's bra. I was the forward motion. Being a guy means being the escalator.

The girls touched each others's breasts tentatively.

"You don't have to be gentle," I said to Kate.

"Oh yeah?"

"Yeah," I said. "Right, Melissa?"

She nodded: I was repeating the words she'd said to me.

Kate kept at Melissa, like she knew how to handle girls. I turned on the little $100 Sony video recorder sitting at my desk. No one paid attention to its chime or eye. Things were getting to the point where none of us would pay attention to anything short of life-threatening danger: we were on the verge of life-affirming pleasure.

Kate Everett

Melissa wasn't 100% in it, and I didn't know why. There were possible reasons: the inevitable framed, arty photograph of a nude woman hanging on Scott's wall. Not enough girl-on-girl excitement. Too much to drink. By all of us. It had been four months since I was last with a girl— an on-again, off-again girl named Sabrina who, like me, had that night in college that made her think maybe she wasn't solely into guys.

Then Sabrina picked a guy over me and pretty much broke up with me. My big thought was, Fuck you, Sabrina. A couple days after, Clint and I were in Caffe Vita when he told me this graphic but hot story about a girl from *The*

Stranger's online dating site. I was intrigued. It took me another week to make the profile. I was too young for online dating, but so what? Getting some is almost always better than not getting some. I'm like a guy in that way. I like to be seduced, but when I need to, I can make the decisions and keep my mouth shut.

Scott Sole

Melissa felt unlike herself, like she'd calibrated her body based on what she'd seen in porn, which related to real sex about as much as TV shows featuring outer space did to walking on the moon. She was drawing on the principal of an account she'd forgotten she opened. She was exhausting my well-developed ability to analogize.

She was all frenzy, and I didn't know how frenzy related to pleasure. She was so different, glistening with sweat and feeling Kate's body, than she was in the classroom, wrapped and sealed. The alcohol made her drier than usual, and we used much Babelube from Babeland. She wouldn't stop. She was determined in a way I'd never seen. But determined to do what? To prove what?

Kate was fully devoted to her craft. She accepted direction when I pulled her hips up and pushed her face, gently but firmly, into Melissa. I admired Kate's way of sussing what Melissa might have really wanted, of reacting to everything Melissa's body asked for. But I didn't really know her beyond the bedroom. She lived for the bedroom; I wished I could too. At one point she whispered to me, "Some women respond to the kiss, some to the whip." I wanted to know which she was, but she didn't reply.

Night passed to morning and Melissa finally passed out. A double bed wasn't an easy place for three. Kate and I were on opposite sides of the girl of the hour, and I sensed that we were likely, on some level, to stay that way.

"I thought that went well," I said.

"That's it?" Kate said. "It went okay? You have the passion of a man who just made an omelette and didn't overcook it."

"When something is great, you don't have to say it's great. In college I had a writing teacher who said, 'Don't draw a picture of a horse then then write "horse" under it.' His point was that if you can't tell that it's a horse, the drawing is shit."

"You wrote 'horse' under it."

"Okay, okay, that was the most spectacular, amazing, incredible threeway of my life, a sexual experience that most men can only dream of, I feel complete as a human being, I was taken to heights of ecstasy unlike anything I have ever known or ever will know. The heavens fell, the seas crashed, the night became day and the day became night."

"You sound insincere."

"That's why I said at first that it went well."

"It did," Kate said. "You were sensational."

"Thanks for flattering me. I was the extra man."

"Men are surprisingly extraneous, yes."

"To you, maybe. Not to Melissa."

"Are you so sure?"

Melissa was the first one up and out of bed. By the time I stirred, she was mostly dressed. By the time I was cognizant enough to ask if she wanted breakfast, she'd picked up her heels and her panties were no longer hanging from the closet door handle. Women hate the word "panties," as I learned too late to salvage one relationship. Everything is education.

I checked the alarm clock next to my bed: 8:25. Around the time second period started at Herbert. Melissa had only slept for a few hours.

"You okay?" I said.

"Yeah."

"Come back to bed."

"I've gotta go."

"Where?"

"Scott," she said. "How many times have you done … this?"

"A gentleman never kisses and tells. Come back to bed. The bed is this way. Where are you going?"

By the time I said it, she was already quietly closing the door to my room. Even slinking out, her courtesy was exceptional. Like when she was a student. She'd make a great teacher.

Next to me, Kate groaned.

"What was that about?" she said.

Melissa Leon

I went back to look at the damn post again, dressed and humiliated. The more I heard about Scott—his posts, his going to *Rocky Horror*—the more outrageous he seemed. Did he really think he could get away with all this?

Scott hadn't even offered the hook to me. Not that I wanted it, but he didn't offer. Like I wasn't special or pretty enough for it. He'd had all damn semester to make his move on me. I wish I'd dumped my New York boyfriend sooner. I thought I was being obvious with Scott. Not obvious enough, I guess.

A guy I knew in college said women are almost never obvious when they think they're being obvious; obvious to a guy is jamming your tongue down his throat and groping in his jeans. I'd told him he was full of shit, but then I started noticing things differently and thinking, *No, maybe he was right.*

I was tempted to go out to a bar and show Scott he wasn't the only one who could tramp it up.

The picture mesmerized me. Even through the drinks, yes, it was Kate who modeled the hook. She was cute, too, for the right guy, and she's got the butt. The ass. But Kate still didn't have what I had. She was my age, or close. Scott likes them young, I guess, like most guys. She wasn't wearing the same underwear she'd worn for our threeway, and I hadn't spent so much time looking at her nude back, but it was enough. Scott was risking his job—everything. I guess that's part of his life.

Someone chooses a profession as conservative as teaching, where you can track, practically to the minute, how much you'll make from the time you start to the time you croak at 80. Scott was doing something dangerous. If he wasn't willing to take risks, we wouldn't have done what happened. I wouldn't care about him so much, even when I know I shouldn't.

Scott Sole

To say Melissa was angry about the post would be an understatement on the order of "The universe is a big place." I saw her on a bleary Monday after the big weekend. My third period was free, and I usually spent it drinking tea and aimlessly throwing a squeeze ball up and down, pretending to prepare for class. I wanted Melissa on the way up, I wanted Kate on the way down, and in the end I didn't know what I wanted. My heart ran an insurgency against itself.

This time Melissa came in and said hi, then she hissed, which was strange in combination with the way she slid into my class like a woman on a quest for a quickie.

"Scott!" she said. "Are you crazy?"

"Possibly," I said. "Crazy in love? Anything specific making you ask?"

"That—that post."

"The one on Jane Austen? I find her boring, no matter what middle-aged women tell me. I keep that opinion to myself around students, however, because they lack the maturity to understand—"

"No! You know which one."

I made innocent, with big, anime-style eyes. "The one about *Nine and a Half Weeks*? I thought it was risqué, but Elizabeth McNeill is literary enough to defend at a school board meeting. In an age of *Fifty Shades of Grey*—"

"With the—" She raised her arms like Kate. It was like they shared much more than me.

"That's a good look for you," I said. "You noticed it on my wall?"

"What's with Stacy seeing you at *The Rocky Horror Picture Show*?"

"Shouldn't you keep her away from that sort of immoral, corrupting material? Granted, I first saw it when I was 14, and it led to the development of the warped sensibility you know and love today."

"Are you capable of talking to me," Melissa said, "or are you going to talk around me?"

"If we weren't at school," Scott said, "I'd invite you to sit on my lap. Come here, kitten. Purr for me while I rub your belly."

"This is serious!"

"Behind your ears, then? Many women find that space to be an erogenous zone."

"Did you hear me?"

"Fine, fine," I said. "Let's be serious, despite my allergy to seriousness. If I break out in hives, ask Lola for her EpiPen. Did you know she's allergic to bees? Okay: the things we did. You weren't bothered this weekend. Why worry now? By the way, did you know I wrote a sex advice column in college?"

"You need to be more worried."

"Why? Knowledge shouldn't be dangerous. If I don't stand up for the truth, who will?"

"Dan Savage. You're not a martyr."

"If not for him," I said, "I might not've been able to post the Safe Zone sign."

"Scott!" Melissa said. "This is not—"

"Yeah, yeah, I'm aware of the perils of a straight college guy writing about a subject in which he lacks experience, but I wrote it with a girl, not to worry—"

"It's like you have a death wish."

"Freud would agree. If so, however, it's unrelated to my thirst for knowledge. The pictures were rather tame. No nipple. I follow the same rules as network TV. Did you read it? The post, I mean?"

"Several times."

"Think it was hot?"

"This is ridiculous."

"It is. We're living in Seattle, not some terrible, godforsaken place like Missouri, where hypocrites rule the land

and think a person can still be a virgin after taking it up the back door. Texas might be transitioning. I hear Austin is nice."

"You're impossible," Melissa said. "My sister, Arianna, and Sheldon all know. If they know, everyone at Herbert will shortly."

"Yeah?" I said, and I stopped tossing the ball and abruptly swiveled to stare deep into Melissa's eyes, like the hero with a thousand faces. "What can they do to me?"

Melissa Leon

No one expects their little sister to bring them juicy gossip about an older man they've had a fling with, but life brings surprises. More than a fling, really. When I graduated from Herbert, I never thought I'd return as a teacher; when Scott introduced me to Kate I didn't think she would have the ability to manipulate me like she did. Or that I loved Scott as much as I did without being able to say it. We'd been flirting all semester. Hadn't we? Hadn't we, despite the guy I was hanging onto when I first moved back? I thought Scott would wait around, being an option for I don't know how long. The good ones get taken fast.

I had an idea that he was dating around without being too loud about it, just like I had an idea that Lola Messina, the improbably sexy French teacher who should really wear higher shirts and lower skirts, crushed on Scott as hard as some of his former students. As hard as I had.

I don't know what it was about him. You rarely do with guys. They all seem alike until one pops out and you're like, *This one*. But if you ask yourself, *Why this one*, you can make up reasons, none real—they're merely rationalizations you've come up with, *ex post facto*. Scott was average looking—average height, average size, straight brown hair, a loose walk like he might trip himself. Maybe it was the intensity of his focus: when he worked on an essay one-on-one, he asked sharp questions. For those moments you were the only thing out there. Guys, fuck, they look at you and only wonder what you look like nude, which gets them thinking about their exes nude, which gets them thinking about Internet porn … Once they know you nude, they look past you, wondering about how the team is doing this season. With Scott, yeah, you'd get that impression sometimes—he's a guy—but not all the time. He was so good with the language. Words. Most teachers want five boring paragraphs. He wanted you to sound right. Closer to music than writing.

If I'd been able to, I would've started things with Scott— Mr. Sole, then—much earlier. But I wasn't as confident then as I am now. Scott gave me the hammer and nails to build that confidence.

Melissa Leon

Five years ago, during the spring of my senior year, I'd broken up with Mark Malone. I mean, he broke up with me to sleep with Irina Upton, which I should've known when he stopped wanting to have sex. Sex with me, every spare moment, that is. Life's first true adult problem feels like someone just hit you from behind. When a guy's interest in sex drops like a thermometer in October, worry.

It pains me to think about how contingent a guy's interest is, how that contingency is based on my body, but the world is what it is and guys, the jerks, are who they are. Including Mark, a teenage boy but basically a guy who was my first real breakup. No, worse than a breakup: My first real heartbreak. He told me Irina was hotter than me. I responded with waterworks, eating disruptions, thoughts, fantasies about a poetic death.

A week later when Scott and I were putting the newspaper to bed there was this moment when we looked at each other, like the movies, the conversation about picas and subheads dying while I waited for what I thought was coming. I was aching for a kiss when he moved away.

Nothing happened that time or the time after that; I'd take the bus home and furiously masturbate about what hadn't happened.

Scott knew what was wrong when Mark dumped me. He said college would be different (it wasn't, not entirely), Mark was a temporary setback, I would find someone else. I didn't understand then that real learning doesn't occur during class. It happens in the halls and between the lines.

"You know what I need?" I'd said. "A more mature man."

"How mature?" he'd said.

"Someone done with college. With a job, of course. A future. And a nice smile. And—"

"A real job, or will penniless DJs do, as they will for most girls after a drink or two? So many girls, they say they want one thing, then they go out to drink so they can disconnect themselves enough to find what they really want. Long, unreasonable lists about requirements go away in the moment."

"I want a real guy."

"Bet you'll find one," he'd said, "soon as you graduate."

PART II

Sheldon

To understand me, Arianna, and Stacy, you have to go back a couple years, to shit I don't usually talk about anymore. Somewhere between the time I began searching for Internet porn and the time I got to high school, I got to thinking about making it myself. I mean, why not? David Hsu was building his own cell phone apps. Sarah Willard had a band and was uploading her crappy music. She sounds like a dying frog. I seriously don't think I've met someone with that little talent and that much delusion. Point is, you want something for yourself, you make it for yourself. Simple as that.

Herbert had assemblies about how it's illegal to take naked pictures of yourself or anyone else under 18. Big fucking deal. I'm naked in the shower every day and haven't been arrested for it. Yet. Besides, my dad would buy the baddest lawyer in Seattle. If they arrested every girl who sent a picture of her boobs to a guy, we wouldn't have any cheerleaders.

When I was in middle school, before I knew anything about girls, my brother Thomas told me that high school girls were easy: you just gave 'em a bone and that made them happy. He said it with his girlfriend right there. She laughed with him. That moment told me about possibilities.

If I had to pinpoint a moment when it started, I would have to pick right there.

It's harder and easier to get girls to do it than you'd think. You have to get them to imagine it's their idea. If you touch them on the forearm or shoulder, they're more likely to. I want to work in Hollywood one day. Everyone will know who I am. Arianna thinks the same thing, but I'm smarter than her. I have a real shot. I'll do what I have to to break in.

Stacy was really hot, no matter the deal with her face. The trick was making her worry that she's not. Thomas told me that too. He used to be friends with Arianna's brother, James Stephenson.

When I told him about liking Arianna, he laughed and said, "Been there, done that."

If he could, why not me?

Scott Sole

When she was a senior Melissa didn't write as well as she could have. Few high school students do unless they have uncommon personalities combined with a skilled editor. But she was so much better than most other students that I paid too much attention to her. Students will notice favoritism. Teachers notice talent.

Melissa's work in creative writing had a fantastical, fizzy quality that was bound up with its probably imagined descriptions of sex and sexuality. Most high school students wisely avoid the topic most on their minds or address it obliquely through such dense symbols that they might've been Nathaniel Hawthorne's contemporaries. But her stories were so stark that I couldn't help but imagine they were based on extensive experience. How much of the sometimes very frank writing came from things she'd done? How much of it was flirtation on the page?

Melissa Leon

I'm sorry I caused Scott so much grief. At the time it seemed like nothing at all, since we waited until after graduation. But he changed me forever, and the days after graduation were some of the best of my life.

Scott Sole

When I began to know Melissa as more than a face in the crowd, she was starting that phase women go through as they suddenly realize, "I could sleep with almost anyone I want, any time I want." I don't know what takes them so long—perhaps it's because they get in a paradox where they think the guy they most "want" is the guy they don't think they can "have" for some half-ass reason.

In college, I challenged my friend Natalie this way: what would her male friends do if she showed up in their beds wearing nothing but lingerie?

"But we're still friends," she'd said. "Just friends."

"No," I'd said. "You only think you're friends. Would Leo pass the lingerie test?"

"I don't know."

"You don't want to admit it. Virtually all straight guys would fail the lingerie test."

"Not all of them!"

"If women wanted to, they could bed a new guy practically every night by smiling. Most of them simply don't want to, or they don't believe the guys they're around are like that."

"Oh. But—"

"But nothing. It's true. That's what women don't understand about men, and men don't understand the sheer number of offers women get and don't want."

As a first-year teacher I had practically the same conversation with Melissa, only replacing "Leo" with "Mark," her ex-boyfriend, who broke up with her for predictable reasons. At the time I'd wanted to lie to Melissa and say that things got better, people became kinder and less shallow as they grew up, but if anything the opposite was true. Romantic veils were pierced by boredom, by want, by drive, by evolution, by fear. Adults are better at dissembling but their motives aren't fundamentally different from teenagers.

Through the spring of her senior semester, Melissa looked for reasons to be alone with me. I didn't resist as much as I should've. One major thing saved me: girls simply will not make the first move. They'll put themselves in a position to have the first move made but will rarely make it. They don't have to.

Melissa would find me in the newspaper room. She knew I'd hang out at Stumptown, so she'd send me texts when she "studided" there. She'd work late on the paper.

She'd bring her short stories to me. She must have expected something to happen, but the mind of a teenage girl doesn't disentangle ideas. Melissa was just a girl who was figuring out what it meant to be a cute girl. Being a cute girl has its pleasures, with guys watching wherever you go and offering you things.

Melissa Leon

Scott isn't the kind of experience you forget; if he were, the Kate thing wouldn't have cut like a knife across the face. I didn't think it would bother me so much, watching him with another girl, and she showed me I wasn't the girl I thought I was and that I still wanted Scott, wanted him to hold me, wanted him to talk to me about art and good drinks and how life works. Though I'd never admit it, he still sometimes provides the grist of fantasies before bed, assuming there isn't someone in bed to provide more than fantasy. Sometimes Scott's face still floats in front of me even when another man is inside me.

In high school I was pretty sure we'd sleep together. I wrote stories to nudge and inspire him. He was on my mind all the time, when I should've looked for guys closer to my own age. He did give me some oblique romantic advice. In high school too many boys were everywhere, yearning for girls who look for them. Problem is, they don't know what to do when they get you. When I was a junior, Scott told me to smile at boys and say hi, and they'd often do the rest. He was right, although their level of skill was lower than their enthusiasm. Why didn't I know that when I was younger? Why didn't I know so much when I was younger?

One time, in maybe April of my senior year, we were sorta leaving Dream Club together—Dream Club is what Herbert called the book group, as if "Dream Club" was somehow less nerdy than "book group." We'd been discussing *The Angel's Game*, and I was heavily identifying with Isabella's literary ambitions and her desire for Martín, the sexy, troubled older writer and her cutting when she'd been nude, standing poetically on the balcony with the light behind her.

Scott and I weren't *really* leaving together—I actually sort of stopped near the door, thinking we should casually walk out in tandem. When he got up from the crappy, falling apart chair behind his desk, my vision blurred into lurid fantasy inspired by Zafón and *The Story of O* and Sasha Grey.

I kept expecting him to slide his hands around my hips and grab my ass to pick me up. The vision was so wild and powerful that I must have blushed because he immediately stepped away, like I might be catching. I wore those tight black leggings that make my ass a jiggling target. The only downside: I can't see the guy's face as he watches me walk away. But I like it. Girls know he's looking. Oh, we know. That or he's gay.

The vision dissolved when he spoke and we pulled back into the classroom. He was speaking about college instead of what was on my mind: sex.

"Have you heard any other offers yet?" he said.

"Yeah," I said. "Colgate, Clark University, Brown, and Whitman. But I *hate* waiting." I put a finger in my mouth, just a little tip on the side, without totally thinking about what Mr. Sole must have been thinking. He was mature enough to ignore it, which I hated and was glad for.

"Planning to visit?"

"Yeah. My dad's going with me. But Colgate and Clark had pretty sweet financial aid offers. Whitman, kind of. I guess I have to decide. The NYU offer is weirdly nice."

"Money matters," he said.

"What would you do if you were me?"

"If NYU is giving you substantial financial aid, picking them would be tempting. They're known for being stingy with aid, too—plenty of people will pay whatever it takes to live in New York. You do realize the game all these schools are playing, right?"

"I don't think so."

"It's like buying a car. Schools have a sticker price that's supposed to make you go, 'Damn, I can't afford that.' You apply, they offer discounts. The more attractive the applicant, the bigger your discount. You'll get bigger discounts at less prestigious schools. Brown basically didn't offer shit, right?"

"Right. That's really nasty."

"The world isn't very nice, however good its PR. Only good people make it tolerable. One point. Brown's an Ivy League school, so it doesn't give real merit money because it doesn't need to. Plenty of rich parents will pay for the privilege, even more than'll pay for NYU. The vast middle get left out."

"What should I do? I could still go to UW." And stay here, with you, and spend lazy Sunday mornings in your arms.

"Only if you want to," Scott said. Did he know that I carefully took proximity to him into the decision? "Don't you want to try new things?"

"Yes," I said.

We had another waiting-for-a-kiss moment that I was thought was going to happen. Then someone approached.

It was Lola Messina, the French teacher all the boys liked for obvious reasons and because she taught them the word *fesses*, and Marcus Stanislaw, the school cop, who was as young as Scott but dangerous-seeming, like the bad kids he was supposed to protect us from. He had a smoothly shaved head and wraparound shades. Herbert is a nice high school, not a drug sting.

"Mr. Sole," Marcus said, drawing out the words. "I do believe we have an arrangement this fine evening. Unless you are busy."

"No," he said. "Just finishing up."

"You sure?" Ms. Messina said. "If you're, uh, occupied, we could go on our own."

"Leave you be," Marcus said.

My face got hot. I could handle the other kids. This was different.

"No, no," Scott said. "Unless you have any other questions about that, uh, essay, Melissa?"

"None," I said, picking up and liking the lie. "Thanks so much for your help. It's really—great."

"Scott is great," Ms. Messina said. "Aren't you, Scottie— excuse me, Mr. Sole."

"I'll be going," Scott said.

"We'd love to invite you, honey," Marcus said, "but we're going to an establishment of an adult nature."

They laughed while I picked up my backpack and Ms. Messina was like, "Careful, Marcus, that's how we all get into trouble."

"You an expert in trouble, huh?"

I left as Ms. Messina was kind of saying in that smoothly medium voice of hers that she could make sound like a bark or a lover's, depending on need, "Scott, about that girl with the crush—"

But the door shut and I didn't hear anything else or want to think anything else about Scott going to the bar with his friends, where he'd meet someone, someone with a tight office blouse and a pencil skirt, with hair done and adult moves.

Scott Sole

When Melissa left, Marcus studied her bobbling ass as she walked. Lola had this new bar she wanted to try, one that was too expensive for teachers' salaries. She had a way of getting her way when she wanted it.

"Scottie," Lola said, "Does that girl have a serious, 'Don't Stand So Close To Me' thing?"

"No, no," Marcus said. "*You* got a crush, man?"

"Marcus," Lola said, tapping her lip, sexy, "you may have a point. Scott looks so guilty. Like he's already done the crime. Have you had a taste you're not supposed to? Come on, we're going."

"I don't know if I'm up for it today," I said. "I should grade these *1984* essays."

"Excuse me while I say: Fuck that shit. Grade them like your students wrote them."

"First round on me," Marcus said. "You in?"

"Let's be honest. Of course I am."

"Only if you tell," he said, like he already knew, "what you and that fine woman were speaking of."

• • •

Melissa Leon

On graduation day, I was smiling with my friends—the few who were left— and fantasizing about my "inappropriate" crush. It's lonely being a senior girl without a boyfriend. No other girls want to be friends, and every day consists of waiting for college and for life again, with better guys who care about something other than sports and video games.

Scott was there, as he'd promised. I was wandering in heels that made my feet hurt, but when I saw him I practically ran to hug him, leaving my family behind.

He saw me coming and braced like he was going to do a squat, which let him pick me up by the hips and give me a quick twirl. He'd done that sort of thing in salsa, but never like this, and I felt so alive and laughing at getting the hell out of Herbert.

My family was there, which made it awkward when I felt myself getting wet when Scott and I hugged. But I did something I'd never done before but have done many times since: asked him to text me. To go out. If I didn't it would never happen. With a lot of guys, especially younger guys, if no one does anything no one gets laid, right? Most girls won't say the straightforward thing. I'm not most girls.

He said, "What're you doing tomorrow?"

"Recovering from the senior party."

"Rough. What about the day after?"

"Nothing. But tomorrow works too. Try me then."

He did.

• • •

Scott Sole

Keeping your job is more important than telling the truth or acting on crushes. But I was a young teacher and Melissa was so blatant. Even with her pursed pouty lips in my mind I almost didn't call about dancing. Some sort of line was clearly being crossed, but I saw her posing with the diploma that pronounced her done with high school. Who am I to stand in the way of happiness?

Melissa Leon

Scott knew someone spinning at the Alibi Room. We agreed to meet about a mile from my parents' place in Capitol Hill. I changed my outfit four or five times. I mean, I knew how to wear a flaring salsa skirt, but should it be white? Black? Pink? Did it matter? Underwear? I went with a white skirt, but I kept touching it, hoping it wouldn't get dirty. Hoping for but not ready to articulate what I hoped for, for what we all hope for.

It was only nine when I took off, but my parents were like, "Where're you going?" and I didn't want to tell, so I said "Out with friends" and was gone, fast as Mark when we first started at it.

Scott was waiting for me like he'd promised, at Pike and 28th, near a sushi place and Voila, the French bistro. I could imagine him taking me there, me being very sophisticated and him ordering wine while speaking, for some reason, French, even though I was pretty sure he only knew English.

"Hey," he said.

"Hey," I said.

He started to say something else and stopped. Sometimes you don't have to talk. We hugged, and he traced my arm, pausing to grasp twice. I was pretty sure from the way he was smiling at me, a little goofy, that he liked what I'd picked to wear.

We might've talked some about our summer plans—I wasn't really paying attention. The night was cool but nice. I should've brought a jacket. I could see Scott thinking about whether he should put his arm around me.

They were checking IDs at the Alibi Room's door, but Scott went up to the bouncer and said hi. They shook hands and the bouncer waved (and waived) us in.

"You want a drink?" Scott said.

"Uh, sure," I said. No one had ever offered me an adult drink. A drink like an adult, I mean. It made me feel sophisticated and uncertain and like sex in equal measures.

"Hang on. It's easier for me to do the ordering."

I didn't know what to do. There was a worn dance floor with maybe a dozen people on it and small round tables like jellyfish, some pushed together to form mega tables. Neon signs advertising beers were on the wall. Old road signs were hanging; my favorite said "Speed Humps" like you'd normally see "Speed Bumps."

A guy with kind of greasy hair in a pony tail came up and asked me to dance. I did, and his skill on his feet almost made up for the rest of him. He liked cross-body leads more than he liked doing anything with them. Halfway through I caught a glimpse of Scott leaning on one of those jellyfish tables next to the dance floor, holding two cups of reddish liquid. I smiled at him. He didn't smile back. There was a chick next to him, talking. When the dance was done I wanted to leap into his lap, but I restrained myself as he passed the cup. The woman left.

"Vodka cran?" I said.

"You a frat party regular?"

"No! I just—you know."

He smiled. "I do. The drinks here are terrible. But the atmosphere's nice."

He began a dirty story about a female friend of his who consumed too many vodka cranberries one night in college, ultimately involving a man named Tye Crum. Never trust a person with two one-syllable names. For an hour we danced without saying much. Scott wasn't quite as good a dancer as he thought, but he was fun and liked it, and that made me like it. I'd overheard him say that if you're good on your feet you'll be good on your back.

"Let's get out of here," he said, "have a drink at my place."

He didn't ask: he took my hand and threaded our way out. On the street he began texting, and when I tried to look over his shoulder he pivoted to block me.

"Tut-tut," he said. "Privacy still counts for something."

"Who're you texting?" I said.

"Roommate. Don't mind me."

Like someone else talking I heard myself say, "Not yet."

The Uber was too long and too short and the first real kiss, instead of being magical, was done at an awkward angle across a backseat where we couldn't get our hands properly involved. We broke off and held hands until we got to Scott's place, where we made out on the stairs.

Inside Scott turned momentarily shy. Back then his place was dingy, but not dingy enough to turn me off the thoughts of sex. Eventually standards emerged, and the cobbled-together leavings of friends and relatives and IKEA—little more than a spot to crash and have sex—were less attractive. Later, when I was in college, I realized that it was much better than it could've been. Men really are pigs, where they live, and then they're surprised when women aren't interested. Clean up and hit the gym and it's not so hard.

On the brink we were able to pretend we were just friends, shadows who hadn't solidified. Then things began to happen. He spent a long time locking his door. When he turned, he didn't do anything at first. Then put his arms around me in one smooth motion to begin kissing me. I really liked that. It was over much too soon, like the stairway makeout.

"You want another drink?" he said.

"Sure," I said, because he asked.

It was so different than with Mark, my high school boyfriend, who would be rushing to get me undressed and home before curfew, before his parents came back—before, before, before. With Scott I felt the absence of time's press. I wanted to keep kissing, and I badly wanted for us not to be in the kitchen with the splotches on the stove and forgotten pans on the back burners.

Scott made some kind of drink with rum and lots of sugar in it by shaking the ingredients and pouring them into glasses. Mine tasted fizzy.

I took a second sip, and he put down his drink.

"What are we doing here?" he said.

He took mine from my hand. From six inches away he looked into my eyes. He kissed me again, and he ran his hands down my legs and just under my skirt, so he could grab my hips and lift me to put me on the counter for a kiss. He said, "We shouldn't do this." I didn't say anything. It was so much better than being stuck on a laundry machine at a party, like Mark had liked.

I didn't know what to do with my legs, but Scott did. He grabbed them and wrapped them around his back. Only the shift of his lips and tongue existed, and those feelings in my body. Then he picked me up, this time totally under my ass, touching me and turning me on, and carried me into the bedroom, grabbing a blindfold along the way.

Scott Sole

When you're doing something you know you're not supposed to, no matter how right it feels, you feel nerves no matter how else you feel. Nerves should convey sensations, not be sensations. I didn't immediately embrace Melissa, though she knew what she was there for, and I knew that she knew I knew. There would be plenty of time to admire my copy of *The Guide to Getting It On* afterward. Plenty of time to admire hardbacks, much read, of Carlos Ruiz Zafón and Elmore Leonard. We can't think about those things clearly with so much sex and its promise in the air. It's hard to mix a drink when you're thinking about her naked and she's thinking about you naked, inside her.

I'd never done something this forbidden. Not when I snuck out of my parents' house as a teenager. Not when I'd gone to erotic parties with a college girlfriend. It was as close as I'd ever get, or want to get, to the Dimmesdale experience, Melissa with a look of utter absorption few teachers see on the faces of their students.

Melissa felt like a rush for orgasm. She must have been used to doing it in tight times and spaces, and unused to hours of freedom in a man's apartment. To making it a leisurely pleasure, not a race, though both had their pleasure.

Most women tend towards leisure and long build-ups, but urgent fucking has its place, for variety. I somehow finished first, the first round, and then used my tongue.

In an interlude she said, "Do you know how many times I've thought about this?"

"No," I said, thinking of how many times I'd thought about this. "And don't tell me."

The next morning I woke up thinking about what Melissa had whispered to me the night before, when her legs were wrapped around me and my hand was in her hair, pulling in time with her sex noises: "Sometimes forbidden fruit is the sweetest."

It was an improbably sophisticated statement from a woman of her age.

Melissa Leon

That summer we had sex at least once day. Twice occasionally, sometimes three. My parents knew something was up and pressed me to bring him over after work. Whoever he was. I was stuck in a coffee shop, slinging espresso for thirty hours a week—I hadn't managed to get a lifeguard gig—and the rest of the time I didn't want to spend in my family's home. I wanted to spend those true hours in my boyfriend's arms. No: lover's arms. I'd thought enough to think myself into wanting a lover more than a boyfriend. A lover made me wonder why I'd bothered living before.

In early August I looked at Scott after a marathon session when we'd experimented with straps, blindfolds, and fuzzy handcuffs. I had curled into a parenthesis, feeling utterly exhausted like school had never made me. Scott formed the other half.

"I could do this forever," I said. "Why do I have to leave?"

"Because everyone grows up. You say you could do this forever, but have you had a real boyfriend before?"

"Mark," I said. "Not sure if he counts. The other guys, definitely not."

"I know the answer should be no, but I want to check—was I your—first?"

I didn't shake my head immediately. He wasn't my literal first, in the sense that I'd done the deed before, with Mark, and a long time before without him. They didn't last. In bed or outside it.

Scott went on, "A lot of us don't have one first. I didn't. You should have your nominal, official first, and then the first person you really explore, both their body and mind. That's when you get good. Not the first time you score a basket, but the first time you realize you can really play a full game. People get all worked up about the first time when they should be thinking in totally different terms."

"Your firsts were how different?"

"Different enough. Point is that life makes you grow up, things change, and if we had this crazy affair for a year or two, you wouldn't feel about it then like you do now. Better to feel it so good and let it go."

"Yes, I guess, I would stay. I wish I hadn't picked NYU."

"Sometimes life brings you upon a choice you don't want to make, and those choices often happen at the intersection of romance and school."

"Talk dirty to me, baby," I said.

"Okay, okay, I know. Remember you're lucky. All of college can be like this, if you learn to flirt. So many girls are lousy at flirting. The ones who get the guys they want aren't

JAKE SELIGER

always the prettiest or hottest or whatever. They're the ones who know how to work it. How to flirt. They're the ones who've become so practiced that it's natural."

"Well," I said, stretching, letting him see me. I reached down to touch myself again. He liked that. "You're slow, but it worked on you."

Scott Sole

"Slow," I said, "or cautious?"

"Oh please," Melissa said. "We kept having those moments, and you kept chickening out."

"You were a student. I like my job."

"I would've never told."

"That's one of the lies everyone tells."

"What're the others?"

"I won't come first. Of course it's real. I'll always love you. Count on me. I'll never leave you. The money is in the bank." I paused, reaching for words, which might be harder for word people like me. "We are all empty words, over time."

"Then shut up and let's do this."

Teaching in front of the class translates well to teaching on your back. Fortunately, it wasn't long before Melissa and I were just doing. Melissa didn't take long to stop being nervous and realize she could try whatever she wanted. That girl blew out the senses, like dancing or music. With her there was no time. Only her and me, alone among billions of other people, behind closed doors, the initial dancing done to conclusion.

The tricky thing was being seen in public. I wasn't doing anything wrong, but I didn't necessarily want the whole world to know about us. I had enough problems. Worry requires imagination, and I was very worried about what people would find out.

Another problem, also regarding knowledge: my friends began to know. Ryan was among them, then.

All my friends who ferreted the truth about Melissa also gave promises not to tell anyone, but that was like telling a cat to stay out of the tuna on the counter. Oblique Facebook comments were posted and duly deleted. Women especially are good at figuring who is with who in that way. In general I denied or evaded. A would-be novelist should be an expert in lying. The only person I didn't lie to was Melissa.

Melissa Leon

Scott and I spent practically the whole summer together, much of it in public. Dancing. Going to the Belltown sculpture park, sometimes at night, with a bottle of wine, on the grass, with no one else around. There were close calls. I didn't care.

Not long after the first time, I'd whispered to him, "You don't have to be gentle, you know," and that got him to do what I wanted.

In August, right before I left, I marked him with hickies to wake him up. Scott had this habit of floating away while we had sex. It made me angry. He'd still be reacting with what I now realize was technical skill, but I could sense that his mind was elsewhere. On the novel he said he wanted to write? The software startup he talked vaguely about founding, to get out of teaching and make real money? I tried so hard to anchor him to the earth, to the bed he was sharing with me. His bed. The first adult man's bed I'd inhabited. Being with a man is an experience. The more he drifted, the more inaccessible he seemed, the more I wanted him.

When Scott was behind me I couldn't see his face, and when I couldn't, I didn't know. Before, I'd always wanted, no, *needed*, to see the guy's face. With Scott I surrendered. He would also always reach one hand around, or let me use a toy, so I almost always finished powerfully at that angle, often with his hand pressing against my lower back. The face thing had something to do with it. That didn't stop me from trying to get his attention via whatever means I had.

Sometimes I'd watch people, mostly men, and wonder what they thought about in their erotic dreams, if they felt as alone and as thrilled as I did. Scott was still young then—23—and I thought most older people only dreamed of staying above water on their mortgage, while I sometimes dreamed about being naked in front of half a dozen men on a boat. Was I the only one?

The girls I knew at Herbert made me think I was alone. Scott told me otherwise and passed me a copy of *Diary of a Sex Fiend*, Zoe Margolis' book. She was British, so it doesn't really count. They can get it on all day in Europe, on the beach even. That's what I thought until I studied abroad in Italy. The fantasy is better than the reality of louts and morons on Vespas shouting at you.

• • •

Stacy Leon

Okay: I shouldn't have made the video. Let the video be made, I mean. No matter what my parents say I wasn't trying to "get attention." It wasn't really me who "made" it anyway. I never said okay or used the camera. It just... happened. Those out-of-control-can't-stop moments. It's really not my fault. If I didn't say okay it doesn't count. Isn't the fact that the whole school saw it punishment enough? Someone played it at the assembly. The fucking assembly. By "accident," yeah. Five seconds was enough for people to know everything.

Pretty much every girl made it her mission to use me as a punching bag. Arianna didn't and didn't care about the video. Sometimes I don't think she cares about anything. I respect her for it.

I'm sorry about the Arianna and Mr. Sole business. I want to stop by his apartment and see how he's holding up, but for some reason I can't. He's got a new job, Melissa told me. In software? It's probably more fun than teaching, and people said he was great in AP Computer Science, but I couldn't do it, staring at a screen everyday. I need to be outside. Screens have caused me enough problems.

Melissa Leon

We kept seeing each other off and on during NYU breaks. Seattle was "coming" home because of him. More rarely I'd see Mark, my first boyfriend, on the side. He'd matured at UW, turning into a serious programmer and skilled guitarist. Although I fantasized about it, I never actually hooked up with both the same day.

My sophomore year at NYU I dated a shitbag named Rory somewhat seriously. "Somewhat" is about as serious as you can date any guy at a school that's like 60% female. The guys work the numbers. They treat us like fucktoys and we let them. I remember being a freshman and stupidly seeing one guy who checked his texts right before sex like he was looking to trade-up. Kicked him out, and that was it for him with me; he just went to a girl down the hall with pierced nipples. Was I the loser then? At least one person got rocks off and it wasn't me.

In places like NYU, a girl who wants a guy to do more than bang her for three weeks and then mack the next pretty girl in stilettos who totters through the hall, bethonged and tipsy, has to go older. Sometimes very older. I went to parties where two-thirds of the population consisted of carefully coifed girls ready to put out for practically anyone who came along. Half went home alone to their vibrators.

NYU was far away. My relationship with Scott slid. He did the same, courteously, with me. He had tact. We didn't ask about each others' sex lives and we didn't tell. Once a friend at a party declaimed that the best sex comes from crossing lines. He thought it was a clever remark and was the sort of person who seemed to have the most sexual experience with his right hand.

Scott and I understood the terms without articulating them. He expected me to meet someone else: that's what you do in college, or you find a relationship with someone who has the same desires for novelty you do. Scott knew when to hold on and when to let go. He knew that sometimes you had to let someone go to keep them, or to keep the memories of them happy. No one wants to acknowledge that many relationships have ideal lengths. Attempting to extend them is like keeping the Ring in *The Lord of the*

Rings: it irreparably changes the thing being extended, like too little butter spread thin across bread.

Scott and I kept talking. He wrote long, lovely emails; he could be a novelist if he really, really wanted to, if he applied his own lessons about the importance of perseverance. As a junior I called to ask what he thought of my being a teacher. My parents were all rah-rah medicine or law, but money is not a quantifier of character. Law and medicine seem to attract the miserable or make people miserable.

I remember Scott's response when I was on voice with him: "I think you'd make a great teacher."

It made me so happy. At the time, I didn't see the downside.

Scott Sole

Melissa started the Masters in Teaching program at NYU immediately after her senior year, since she wanted to be a teacher and she wanted to be in debt for the rest of her life. She'd spent enough time teaching salsa dancing and editing her classmates' essays to think she could do it over the long term.

But there are downsides. The bureaucracy is stultifying. There's no real upward track. Except to admin, which is truly miserable and utterly impossible. A programmer who is tired of making too little money at one company leverages that experience to make 25% more at another. Teaching as it exists today doesn't work that way.

The only way to make more is to get useless, time-consuming master's degrees—ideally before entering the classroom. But Melissa wanted to.

Her New York-based program had agreements with dozens of other teaching programs, including Seattle University. Students could student-teach for a semester in almost any big city. She told me about her plan, about how it would let her come home, save money on rent, and still live in a big city. The catch was, she said, that she needed to make sure she could get a student-teaching gig.

I remember hearing myself say, "I bet I can help you with that."

Melissa Leon

At some point things change, and family is no longer the center. Going home is no longer fun. When mom offers to make the special pancakes that made a young half-forgotten girl squeal, they are no longer special. They are stifling.

For me, that change began when I was fifteen and got Mark, whose hands trembled the first dozen times he fiddled my bra. Guys are supposed to be so eager but most scare at a live wet pussy.

When I got home from teaching, or student-teaching, I became homesick for my own life despite knowing the economic consequences. I lived with my family for a year to save money: not spending the $10,000 rent would otherwise cost let me pay my own way once I got a permanent job, which was an assumption no one had in my generation. Living with parents after college feels like a holding pattern. The lover I didn't have at some point becomes home. Work became purpose. Family is okay for short periods of time, but I was oriented outward, towards the wide exciting world.

PART III

Stacy Leon

When we were sophomores, like a week before the video thing, Sheldon and I were having lunch at Yoshi Teriyaki, talking shit about whoever, when I said by accident, "Arianna fucking *loved* it when James had his friends over."

"What d'you mean?" Sheldon said, too interested.

"Nothing," I said.

"No," he said. "You definitely mean something. Tell me."

He'd stopped eating the chicken teriyaki.

"What has Arianna told you about your brother and his friends?"

"Not very much."

We kept talking like that until finally I said that Arianna would let James's friends sneak into her room. She said they were all bad in bed but fun.

"I thought so," Sheldon said.

"What?" I said.

"I knew that's what you meant, but I had to know."

"Why?"

He wouldn't say. It innocent at the time. The news put in his head that he could get her to do things.

Scott sometimes said that if we do something, it shows that we wanted to at that time, even if we regret it later. Other people can't really "make" us do anything. He said that people want different things over different timeframes. In the short term, you might want one thing, in the long term, something else, and when you're in the heat of the moment, the short term is pretty sweet.

There's a word he uses. He made us look it up—volition. We all have it, he said. No matter what she says, Arianna had it too. Still does.

Scott Sole

If Melissa had come back single I think we would've gotten together, out of the closet. Holding hands and walking down the street. Not the first couple who'd met the way we did, and definitely not the last. Instead she was dating someone back in New York. When that fell apart—Melissa said he found some other fresh young thing—it was around the time I'd become enamored of the online buffet. I thought Melissa would move on and her attraction to me was based on proximity. Convenience is often romantically underestimated.

She wasn't as emotionally stable as she might've been, and I made things worse through deliberate ambiguity. Kate was the catalyst for renewing our relationship. Maybe Melissa only thought I was desirable because Kate was there as a rival.

• • •

Arianna Stephenson

I don't know why I liked Sheldon. He gets all these girls to do things for him, and then he ditches them. What's there to him? He doesn't play sports. If he was a basketball player I'd understand. Like when he goes out, he always says "Hi, you look like you might be cool" to whoever. Thinks he's a boss.

I wanted him to like me, but he wouldn't, exactly. Most guys are thrilled when I say hi. Sheldon, like, treated me like a toy. I'm such an idiot. I wish I'd known how to say no. When I was with him it was so so hard.

Stacy Leon

When did it start? Maybe a month before the tape. Sheldon was chatting with Dave Karpasky and Ronald Chen in the math wing. He called me over. I shouldn't go when guys call. It was pretty late in the day, and I was wondering what they were doing. They were all wearing UW hats, like they'd already left high school.

"We've been talking," Sheldon said. The other two grinned. "And we wanna know: what should you do with a guy who's got an okay body but, you know, not so much in the face department?"

"I don't know," I said.

"Never had this problem with a guy?"

"Kind of. I guess." No.

"What would you do to solve it?"

"Dunno."

JAKE SELIGER

"You quiet today."

Ronald Chen went, "Told you she's not smart. Grades—whatever."

"Stacy, look at me," Sheldon said. He put two hands on my shoulders. Part of me wanted to leave. Part of me kind of liked his hands, the way he stared at me intent. Like a snake. "What would *you* do?"

"I guess I wouldn't go out with him?"

Sheldon sighed.

"You'd bag him!" Ronald said.

I laughed, kind of, not quite knowing what they meant. "You all guys are dumbasses," I said.

"Now," Sheldon said, "we have an equally important question. What if 'he' was a 'she?' What if you had a girl with an okay body but her face—well…"

My own face flushed. "I'd say you wouldn't deserve her." I untangled myself, but not before he let me go, and kept walking, hoping that I'd make it to the bus stop without their calls of "bagger" lingering in my ear.

Arianna Stephenson

I was crushing so hard on Sheldon that I thought if I did what he asked, he'd be my boyfriend. That of course isn't how it works. If a guy wants to be your boyfriend he says so. If you ask him to and he says anything but yes find another one.

Back then I didn't know that and thought it'd be fun performing—you know? I could be a model, but if I could never eat McDonald's again I'd die.

• • •

Stacy Leon

If I was smarter, I would've ignored Sheldon's bagger comment. Instead it got to me. I wanted to prove to him that it hadn't. A couple weeks after that he texted Arianna a suggestion that she and I kiss and send him a pic. We were at her place, for some reason we couldn't get out—her mom was around?—and we made do with what we had. Arianna had me, I had her, we had Sheldon telling us what to do, and sometimes it's hard to say no to what feels good.

Sheldon told us to take our shirts off and press our boobs against each other, and we did it. When he asked for more, Arianna told him to wait. I didn't like that. I told her I wasn't going to do it. She was crushing on Sheldon and stared at me like I was a mouse.

"What's the most daring thing you've ever done?" She asked.

Nothing, of course. I knew her answer would probably involve the way she lost her virginity to James's friends, though she wouldn't identify the culprit.

Instead of, I don't know, leaving, or something like that, I texted Sheldon to say that he could jack off without our help, and he replied that he was looking forward to the rest of the show: he wanted us to come over to his place as soon as possible.

Ariana began a flurry of texting she didn't want to show me.

"Arianna," I said, "what're you doing?"

"Flirting," she said.

She kept "flirting." I browsed Facebook with that feeling of waiting in a doctor's office growing.

Arianna looked up and said, "We should go. I know how we'll sneak out."

. . .

Sheldon

They texted me from the lobby and I went down to get them, thinking about how I had to start things slowly. It was already midnight. Go straight for the kill and they scare. Arianna was the easy one, Stacy the reluctant follower. Every cool girl has some followers.

My dad was out that night. I offered the girls vodka cranberries. Girls like the taste of the really sweet cranberry juice. A drink makes them think they can say, "The alcohol made me do it." It's their girl get-out-of-jail-free card. My dad says girls who can do brown liquor are keepers. Says the guy divorced.

Stacy didn't really want hers, but Arianna sure did. The first one, the second one, the third one. By the second, she was ready to go, and ready to tell Stacy to go too.

"You know that thing you promised me you'd do?" I said to Arianna.

"Which one?" she said. She giggled. When she's on, she's on.

"You know you know."

She exchanged glances with Stacy. Girls always need to confer with other girls to make sure they think what they're doing is okay. Fuck that, have a good time, get it on.

"He wants us to kiss," Arianna said. "Like we did for his picture."

"Hang on," I said. I had one of those little Sony cameras, one that I'd swiped from my dad, and his Olympus mirrorless. And my phone. Nearly as important as condoms. "Arianna. Grab yourself." I gestured. "For a photoshoot."

"Like this?" she said, putting her hands on her hips.

"No," I said, "like this." I put her hands on her chest. "Slowly, slow."

"Really?"

"Hold." I took some pictures.

"Arianna," Stacy said, "I—I have to go."

"No you don't," Arianna said.

"Girl," I said, "have you ever wanted to be a model? This is your chance. To play model."

"You called me a fucking bagger," Stacy said.

"Hardly." I couldn't hardly believe they were doing this. Stacy didn't want to, but like a lot of girls she's a follower at heart.

"Arianna," I said, "take off your shirt."

She did.

"Now," I said, "kiss."

I pulled out the little Olympus camera. Sure, I could use a cell phone, but why not go for quality?

Stacy Leon

I watched, sick and fascinated, as Arianna did what she was told. As I began to, even though I was protesting inside. Why couldn't they see?

Arianna kissed me first. It wasn't me. She started dancing like a stripper. If you've seen the video, you know what happened next. If you haven't seen the video, you've seen something like it online. I don't know how I became like that. Why I became like that. It… it goes against all my morals. I forgot who I was and by the time I remembered it was too late. But at that moment I would be lying if I said I didn't feel free.

I'd entered a new world. The Internet had spontaneously entered Sheldon's bedroom. I mean, I'd seen Arianna without her shirt on a bunch of times—after gym, in locker rooms, when we were much younger and changing for sleepovers. I'd never seen her like this. Where was a boyfriend to protect me? I'd been looking for him since eighth grade, and all I had was a bunch of hookups where the guys would go around the next school day and whisper that yes, their fingers smelled like tuna after, and I would be so humiliated I'd want to die, but not until I killed them first. Then I'd meet some other boy who seemed so sweet, but it took courage, so much courage, so much wanting, and the next Monday or Friday it'd all start again.

I wanted Sheldon to be that boy, with his straight black hair, nice skin, perfect smile, and, always, the girl following him around. I wanted to be that girl, but with us walking together. I wanted Arianna not to be willing to do what Arianna was willing to do. She was the wild girl, I was the prude friend.

Arianna turned to me and said, "Are you ready?"

"Ready for what?" I said. She only wore underwear bottoms.

"You know." She cocked her head at Sheldon. It was so unreal. Like I was in a TV show and I didn't know my lines.

"Um, I don't know." What happened to the girl who knew every answer in class?

"Good enough," Sheldon said. "Do it."

• • •

Sheldon

Neither of them paid attention to the camera, but they both knew it was there. It was impossible not to. Couldn't believe Stacy was going through. Arianna, yeah, sure. She knows. Stacy, not really. Stacy's never really been touched because she's too scared. Didn't like to lose control but she sure pretended to then.

Stacy Leon

Arianna's tongue was surprisingly warm. Aside from her chest against me, it actually wasn't all that different from kissing boys who'd bothered to shave properly. Her arms weren't all over me like an octopus's tentacles. More delicate. If Sheldon hadn't been there, making me self-conscious, I might've liked it.

Sheldon

I wanted to jump in without wrecking the moment. I was going to be immortal. No one got this, not even the basketball team. Both girls took off their clothes. As much as I wanted them to touch each other, they wouldn't really do it like they should have. When I told them things, I was half thinking about how I'd have to cut the sound during those parts, or cut them.

Arianna was getting much more into it than Stacy, like she'd been waiting for this her entire life.

"Think about how you'd behave if your boyfriend was here," I said to Stacy.

"I don't have a boyfriend," Stacy said.

"You would have a boyfriend if he thought you were a cool girl."

"What's that supposed to mean?"

"You know, the kind of girl who'd do this for him."

"I'm not that pathetic that I need a boyfriend, and my boyfriend wouldn't make me do this."

I almost said the obvious.

"I can't keep doing this," Stacy said. She stopped, grabbed her panties, and pulled them back on.

"I'm getting close," Arianna said. "Don't make me stop now."

"Wait a sec," I said. "I'll help you. Let me get a few more pictures."

Stacy grabbed her shirt and held it to her chest. Like I hadn't had a video camera on everything.

Stacy Leon

The morning after the video I woke up back at Arianna's, long before she did, and began frantically texting Sheldon, begging him to delete it. Anything deleted never existed.

He replied and promised he would.

Never trust a man.

Scott Sole

Last year, Frank Ngyuen, Madison Johnson, and Duke Nelson—two juniors and a senior—were huddled around a phone in the newspaper room, almost adjacent to the door such that they could look up and see someone coming. Nice kids. They were so enraptured by Frank's phone that none noticed me hovering.

Phones were and so far as I know still are forbidden during class. Teachers were supposed to confiscate them on sight. It's yet another way of making us into wardens. I hated enforcing the rules, and when I did, I usually pointedly avoid searching the phone itself. Each phone is a little bomb with the potential to destroy its owner and inflict unpredictable collateral damage with all the force of the authorities who make and enforce cruel rules with little regard for the facts on the ground or real people.

They were staring into it. I slid among them to a chorus of "Hey!" and grabbed it. Technically, teachers are never supposed to touch students. They're radioactive. Or the teacher is. Frank held, momentarily forgetting his training, as if he was going to wrestle the phone away. But I had surprise and turned my back to begin watching the screen. It was a girl who pulled aside her bra to show—yes, a nipple. I sighed and assumed it was generic porn—technically a suspendable offense, but who hasn't seen a dirty movie by the time they're a junior in high school? It's like fighting drinking: futile to forbid fun.

I was about to hand the phone back, since a moment of indiscretion isn't worth the hassles of rule enforcement paperwork.

Something caught my eye. It was a purple bra, like one I'd seen protruding from a tank top. The tank top of someone I knew. I studied, transfixed and horrified. Not horrified by the act—virtually everyone gets naked in front of someone else—but by what it meant for me to witness it.

Yes. One of my students.

• • •

Sheldon

I didn't mean for the video to get out. Or the pictures. They were supposed to be for me, but something like that is meant for friends. Can't be kept from friends. Like weed. Don't bogart the chronic, don't bogart the porn. Shawn came over one day, and when I said something about the video he demanded to see it. I said no but couldn't *say* no.

Another time, not too long after, Ronald Chen and Jeff McGurl were like, "What's up with you and Arianna?"

And I was like, "Nothing." They thought we'd been hanging out a lot, and besides, Shawn told them about how I had it. You can't just hog a thing like that. It's there to be, you know, shared.

So I let them see it. They told a bunch of people. Pretty soon the whispers started even among the losers. One day a bunch of my friends came over after school. It was a Friday, and when my dad came home, he made drinks for a few of us. Frank my favorite nerd came over too, and I bet it was him. I should've never shown him, but I did, and that was my mistake. My bad. You gotta figure a guy like him wouldn't tell.

Any of them could've done it. Remember that, before you tell me how it was all my fault and not anyone else's. No one knows where these things start. Celebrities are our role models.

Next thing I know, I get this note saying Principal Shore-well wants to see me. The bitch.

• • •

Scott Sole

I copied the video on my personal laptop for purposes of investigation.

Although I hated to reinforce idiotic high school hierarchies, it's nonetheless true that Frank, Madison, and Sam were not among Herbert's leaders. None were distinguished or socially connected. I liked them in the drab, unexceptional way of good students who'll be forgotten three months after they graduate. It's possible to spend 53 minutes a day with someone for 180 days, only to have them barely register as more than a stranger passed on a city street.

I didn't hold any of these qualities against them: to judge a person based on their malformed, inchoate 14- to 18-year-old selves is to judge the first draft of a novel as one would the final. In college, my senior thesis was on F. Scott Fitzgerald's editing process. The first drafts showed promise, of course, but the man's sentences! His transitions! By publication, they, and the revisions that made them extraordinary, turned Fitzgerald from one of the innumerable forgotten writers who fall like leaves in autumn, only to be mulched for the next year's growth, into Fitzgerald, the hero of the stupid, doomed romance.

I might not be fairly judging students. Madison could found or join the great startup of her generation, Sam could become a diplomat who prevents a major war, and Frank could become a teacher in my own mold. Still, they were not the kind of students to receive the first, incipient copies of a sex tape. They were among the last.

Arianna was definitely on the tape, and my vote for headless body was Stacy Leon. The guy must have been Sheldon. Why him, I didn't understand. This guy, who resembled a rat in appearance and mannerisms, could get these two cute high school girls to get naked and performing. And that's what it was: a performance, copied in tone and style from similar material on the Internet.

Arianna on the tape, I got. She could be talked into jumping off a cliff. Stacy was stranger, more troubling, and not only because I'd known her sister. She was in line to be editor of the *Hatchet*, a plum even in the age of nasty Facebook gossip.

The video must have gone viral over the weekend. I'd heard some kids talking about it, without even realizing what they were talking about—just *that shocking video* like it was the usual YouTube junk. One day it's the honey badger or music video, the next it's their classmates naked. I wasn't really thinking about how the kids were clustering even more than usual in the hall.

Earlier that day, I'd walked out of class with Stacy, explaining something about a story she was writing, and the crowd parted before us like we were Moses. I don't think Stacy knew then. By the time I knew, she wasn't on Herbert's campus.

Stacy Leon

I somehow got it in my head that Sheldon would be my boyfriend if I made the video. Now I look back and think, "How stupid was I?" If a guy wants to be your boyfriend and you offer him the choice, he'll be your boyfriend. If I had a real shot, I'd blown it the minute I pulled my bra down to cup my breasts.

When Sheldon and those assholes called me a "bagger" I wanted to kill him. Instead, I went home and cried, determined to prove I was sexy.

I did, sort of. No one would watch if they didn't think so.

• • •

Scott Sole

Despite knowing the dangers of looking through a cell phone, I did scroll briefly through; the most unusual text said, "ice my cake, dickboys! I want to feel like a breakfast pastry," but otherwise I didn't find anything remarkable.

Laura Shorewell—Herbert's principal—needed to know because she would know soon if she didn't already. She needed a plan to get in front of the problem. The worst political / media / parent problems are the ones unanticipated. Telling her would make the problem a little bit worse at first, like telling your friend that his wife is cheating on him, but full disclosure can have a prophylactic effect on the person doing the disclosing.

One other person needed to know too.

Stacy Leon

The rumors started in the hall and then I began getting the anonymous texts: "Slut." "Bitch." Worse. So bad I turned my phone off. Turning off your phone is like dying. No one turns their phone off. After fifth period I left.

• • •

Scott Sole

Most erotic activities are ridiculous when taken out of context. A dispassionate observer feels little more than he would for mating fowl at the scurrying and enticement and idle pawing, less than a good engineer for his machine.

I gave the phone back to Frank and admonished him not to use it in class. His prominent Adam's apple bobbled like a goose as he stuttered a promise not to and seeming surprised I hadn't busted his ass. I was supposed to, but what was the point? It wasn't his fault more than dozens or hundreds of other students'. Wasn't anyone's fault, except evolution for making us randy and technology companies for giving us the devices we demand.

Herbert was then still wired. I called Laura's office, slipping out of class so the students couldn't hear. The things students don't know are infinite. Like the things I don't.

Francine, the mummified secretary cursed with an evil disposition caused by inadequate sun exposure, put me through to Laura only after I impressed the situation's urgency. Don't debate next month's menu while the kitchen is on fire.

"Laura," I said, "I think we have a situation."

"What's that?" she said.

I explained, sketching a drawing she'd seen dozens of times before.

"Who had the video?" she said.

"I'm not sure," I said. "I saw it over some shoulders. Sophomores? I was late to class and didn't have time to stop."

"You seriously didn't stop?"

"I didn't realize what it was until I heard some students talking about something they'd seen. Then, in class today, someone left a USB key lying around. I looked and found it there."

"Your story is … strange," Laura said.

"You want me to talk to Stacy?"

"No," she said. "I will. Come down as soon as you get a minute. I was looking forward to a morning without crying. Hillary Wang has been showing up once a week because Sarah Behring has been making fun of her grades."

"Tough."

"Why can't they just get along, Scott?"

"If you think about it, the real question is, who can?"

Stacy Leon

Melissa called me from college. She knew before my parents did, somehow, though she refused to explain. She was a junior and acted like that made her the smartest person ever. Every summer when she came back she wore weirder, more expensive clothes that covered less and less of her body. My dad called her the fashionista. My mom was jealous and tried to hide it.

She told me she knew, it was going to be okay, that I wasn't the first girl to get caught like this and wouldn't be the last. She suggested that I fight back, tell people to fuck off, tell the girls that if they weren't so scared they'd be on the screen next, and the best they can do is hook up with a guy at a party.

Melissa didn't sound like herself. She sounded like someone normal.

It was okay advice, but way impractical. I started crying. Melissa was good about that. When I got done she kept going.

"Stacy," Melissa said. "If you expect nothing from men, you'll never be disappointed."

"That's a horrible thing to say," I said.

"That doesn't make it any less true. Trust me."

"Why? How many guys have you, you know?"

"College is different. That's all I'm saying."

I hated it when she got all superior.

"I want to have expectations."

"Then you'll have to learn to live with disappointment when men invariably don't live up to them."

When we got off the phone I texted Arianna to warn her. In my next class I got a note telling me to report to the principal's office.

Scott Sole

Francine waved me in without otherwise moving. I doubted she'd exerted a single calorie more than necessary in twenty years. She had a mongoose's sense of empathy.

Laura's office door was open. She held a coffee cup with "Yes We Can!" in huge letters across it. Dundas was loitering there too, maybe waiting for a look at the goods. There's a certain amount of scrutiny in these matters that goes far beyond what's warranted by necessary investigations. Prurience is forever.

"So—the incident," I said, like a character out of *The Rocky Horror Picture Show*.

"Was someone hurt?" Laura said.

"No. Not physically."

I hesitated, and she motioned for me to spit it out and hurry up since she had better things to do, like checking email or sending nudes of her own to her husband or lover. She'd gone through a recent, acrimonious divorce that was rumored to have been prompted by her own extracurricular activities. They hadn't made her more empathetic.

I didn't want to be the one to come to her, but I wanted even less to be known as the person who knew and didn't. Sometimes ignorance is best but I could not un-see.

"I found this," I said, brandishing a USB key like a dead rodent or used condom, "in the newspaper room."

Laura appraised me with the skeptical-cop affect that everyone who works in education develops.

"That is the shittiest story I've heard this week."

"For now I'm sticking to it. Look at what you're dealing with first. I mean, I've already told you—but seeing is different than reading or hearing."

"Take off the teacher's hat," Dundas said. "Or remove the stick from—" he gestured toward his ass, like a student would—"here to make your point."

"I should get back to my classroom, because I need to get ready for next period and—"

"Wait," Laura said. "You have time. I'll write a note if you need it."

"Wait with Francine?"

"Scott," Laura said, smiling now for a minute, "you're not a student. Do you expect detention?"

"It's just—when you see it, you'll know."

"This kind of incident," Laura said smoothly, "is only as serious as we make it."

• • •

Laura Shorewell

Mr. Sole stepped out so Dundas Gekowski, who is my assistant principal, and I could review the footage. Normally I wouldn't view the material in question, but if everyone has seen it to the point where teachers are confiscating copies, I really have no choice.

They're so repetitive: one teenage girl trying to entice a boy through awkward, unpleasant means based on moves absorbed through advertising or the Internet is like the next. Girls think their lives are Victoria's Secret ads. I run into enough high school girls like that in the Westlake Center store.

The system works. It must work. I felt bad for the girls involved, I really did, but in these matters it's true: I had no choice but to make calls I didn't want to make.

Arianna Stephenson

Stacy texted me to say the video was out and that she'd just talked to Melissa. Maybe ten minutes after that the vice principal showed up to call me out of class and discuss the matter. I went numb.

At home my parents yelled like a hurricane, first at me then at each other. I thought they were going to go nuts. My dad especially. Reminded me of why I never talk to him. My mom understood better but she gave me this lecture about how boys only want one thing from me, and I was like, *you have no idea*. I couldn't say that, of course. I was thinking, *How about you ask me what I want?*

They got started telling each other they were terrible parents and I might have been across the country. I cried until I thought I couldn't, then cried some more.

I wanted to tell them to let me do my own thing but I knew how they were going to be. I went numb and mumbled. Things became foggy until my mom and dad got called, both of them. The rest of school got cancelled for me while the administration debated what to do. The main thing I remember is them wanting to know if I'd acted on my own and who I'd sent the video to.

My brother, James, was pretty cool. He called me that night. He'd dropped out of college and was working for some "cloud storage" company in Portland. I was in my room, with the pictures of me and all my friends on the wall, with the old trophies from swimming. There was still glitter paint on my walls. The middle school phase. My room's really small. It's all my family could afford.

"Here's the deal," Charles said. "In a couple months, it'll blow over. By the time you get back to school next year, people will've forgotten."

"That doesn't help me right now," I said. I actually had a copy of the video on the screen in front of me. I did look pretty hot.

"Sure it does. It means you don't have to hold out long. You're already halfway through."

"Halfway through what?"

"High school. The day after you graduate you'll be thinking, 'Who cares?' "

"I care."

"Not for long. For now, think about doing other things. Get a job if you can. Get a life."

"How can I do that?"

"You have to learn how to figure things out for yourself."

"How can I do that?"

"You're missing the point, Arianna."

Sometimes I really hated my brother. He didn't have to be such a jerk. He acts like some of my teachers, like he knows everything.

"I thought you were calling to help," I said.

"I was. Am. I'm trying to help you help yourself. You're the only person who can."

"Whatever," I said. "Who told you about it?"

"No one. It's not important."

"Not mom and dad?"

"No. I mean, when they told me, I already knew."

"You didn't watch it, did you?"

"No! Of course not."

Liar.

So he was annoying and kind of useful, like usual.

But he gave me an idea. I remember a friend named Beth Culley posting a status update about how bad she wanted to do this program in Europe, and when I saw it, I wanted to too.

In my room I began searching and found it. The pictures were fabulous. Amazing. It was in Barcelona and focused on European fashion, but it recruited American students if they were fabulous. I read everything I could. Watched the videos cause reading sucks. It sounded magical. Like *Harry Potter* come to life. You learned everything about fashion, but not in boring classes.

I kept reading like I was in a trance. Drama. Glamour. Dresses. Everything I didn't have at home. The deadline for this summer had already passed, but I wanted to go. To get away. To be somewhere cool.

The next morning at school the losers in the hallway did what they did. They didn't even respect me playing varsity volleyball, when I could spike their damn heads if I needed to. Stacy would cry. I would get angry.

That night my dad came home, and I practically gave a presentation: the purpose, the costs, the benefits, the draw-backs (none). He likes to think he's really rational. He likes it when you don't whine.

"If you want to help me," I argued, "let me go to Europe."

"If I could," he said, "I would. Your grades aren't as good as they should be."

"But they're not that bad!"

"A 3.0 in high school is pretty miserable. That's showing up, at best. High school should be like a day job: so fucking easy you can do something else at night. You'll realize that when it's too late"

"Why're you so mean to me? You're worse than the fuck-ing losers at school. It's so unfair!"

"I'm not mean," he said. "The truth isn't mean. You need to learn to negotiate. Life isn't about getting what you want. Next summer, we'll talk. How about this: you get at least a 3.7 next year."

"That's impossible."

"Nothing is impossible if you want it badly enough and you're willing to work for it."

I hate it when adults say shit like that. I'm worried they might be right.

"Next summer," I said. "Like James told me to, I'm thinking ahead. What if I don't get the GPA? I like need to go."

"You don't go."

Scott Sole

After school I texted Stacy to ask if she wanted to talk. And I asked for Arianna's number, since I felt obliged to extend the same offer and didn't want to single Stacy out. Inviting both was the easiest way to avoid charges of favoritism. By then, I'd had long experience in counseling the smarter students through mishaps at the intersection of digital technology and burgeoning sexuality, where a nasty left-hand turn and faulty signaling often resulted in collisions that shocked the drivers—and no one else.

Most teachers wisely ignored that stretch of teenage highway, but to do more than observe traffic from orbit, one has to get on the road. That's what I did, wisely or not, because you can't understand high school students without understanding the often cruel, stupid, and vacuous social structures they make.

If I didn't want to understand those structures, I wouldn't think teaching important. If it wasn't important, I'd be doing something else. A lot of something elses. We call high school students children, treat them as such, expect them to behave like adults, yet demand they suppress the same adult appetites teachers and parents indulge.

If they kill or steal they're adults; if they have sex they're "children." I'd also promised myself that I wouldn't be the one to face a student suicide and wonder why I'd never tried.

The best teachers don't just teach domain knowledge; they show you how to live. That was my saving grace in wanting to talk to Stacy. I knew she, like so many teenagers, was desperate for adult guidance and perspective. Teachers were liberally encouraged not to give it.

Stacy replied with Arianna's number and what I read as a grateful acceptance. I suggested coffee at Stumptown in Capitol Hill, which wasn't too far from Herbert and should remind students of where they'll end up, among flirting hipsters with expensive Mac laptops, not where they are, among adolescent cretins who haven't learned how to be.

Stacy said she'd check with her mother, which instinctively made me inhale, as if in fear of a softball striking my groin. If she told her mother, her mother might tell Melissa about our meeting, though Melissa was in New York, and if Melissa knew, she might draw the wrong conclusions. If I told her *not* to tell her mother, that would look more suspicious than I could afford. An invitation rescinded is far worse than one never sent. A signal issued can't be recalled.

I was doing something slightly dangerous: the wrong accusation can ruin lives. A guy in college, Paul Benedict, had a girl accuse him of rape when they were both freshmen. Nothing happened on the legal front—he said, she said— but he ended up dropping out, joining the military, and not starting school again until he was 25. A couple years after it happened, he got a Facebook message from her, while he was sweating his balls off in the latest oil-rich, institution-poor Middle Eastern country where women have almost as many rights as camels, asking him to let bygones be bygones. She'd only meant to "teach him a lesson."

Stacy got to Stumptown before me. She was uncommonly demure in baggy, dark blue jeans, a green Herbert sweatshirt, dour brown rain jacket, no jewelry. A babysitter, not a junior sexpot. Usually she preferred boots or heels with the stupidly tight, distracting leggings that are popular and infuriating, or, in winter, sweaters of the kind that figured prominently in fantasies and literary descriptions, glitter on her eyes and mouth that drew attention to her face, and shiny necklaces nestled deep in her cleavage that dared you to grab and not let go like a coon on a piece of aluminum.

She dressed like Arianna, despite being so different. In college she might begin to cultivate whatever mind lurked inside her and stop playing the bimbo.

"I hear you've had a… tough day," I said.

"Yeah."

"Laura talk to you?"

"Laura?"

"Principal Shorewell."

"She talked to my mom, then to me."

"Look, I won't ask you about how it happened, because I don't need to know, and, frankly, it's not important now."

"You gonna lecture me?" Stacy said.

"Lecture you? Of course not. I try not to in class, let alone—" I waved my hands. Coffee shops were good. They were normal. She'd do dumb time in them as a college student, if she was like Melissa.

"Then… why're you here?"

"To tell you that, no matter what happens, this is going to pass," I said. It was a lecture, actually. "All this stuff is going to go away. No one will care. Life will go on. Don't do something stupid or dangerous."

"I won't," she said. "I promise and, I mean, thanks for the talk."

"Good. I've seen bad coping behavior before. Cutters, that kind of thing."

"Yeah. I know."

"Do you?" I said. "It's so easy to get wrapped up in things that don't matter. What *does* matter to you?"

"I don't know. Friends, I guess. My family."

"You and everyone else. So don't disappoint them."

"I already have."

"Not so much as you think—this thing is personal. In three years you'll laugh about it at Thanksgiving." I couldn't tell her there that her sex life was mostly her business, not her family's, as long as she didn't get pregnant. "Work forward from here. Meaning, survive the idiots at school who are your classmates."

An espresso whistle blew. Stacy sipped her cappuccino. We were sitting next to each other along a bench, maybe a foot apart, knees towards one another, torsos away, the better to talk but not be too close.

"Now what?" Stacy said.

"Shut down your Facebook profile for a couple weeks minimum. Yeah, I know, to you that's like telling you to live under a bridge, but you can do without the online harassment."

"I can't delete Facebook!" Stacy said. "And what if it ends up online? Really really online?"

"Your choice about Facebook. Don't say I didn't warn you. The other thing … if it ends up on the Internet, it ends up on the Internet. Your biggest advantage is the needle-in-a-haystack effect."

"Huh?"

"Think about it like this." I pondered how to phrase a delicate truth. "If you've ever looked online for, uh, material that people under age 18 aren't technically supposed to view, and I'm not saying you have, you'll know there's an incredible abundance of it. More is being created all the time. The chances of someone you know, or someone who you *will* know, stumbling across any is reasonably small and shrinking all the time."

"That's good." It also wasn't as true as I would've liked it to be, but I was working on hope and optimism for the time being.

"Right. In that assembly at the beginning of the year, the administration makes you think one picture or video or whatever and it's going to follow you around your whole life. I hate to break it, but there are millions and millions of pictures and videos online."

"Yeah. I still have to go to school."

"For now. I see two main paths for you. One is the standard path: act contrite and pretend you made a great mistake you'll never make again. The penance path, with its Christian roots."

"What's 'contrite' mean?"

"Apologetic, guilty. That's the easy way. The way most people would probably go."

"The other?"

"Dare them to mock you for the things they'd like to do themselves, if they were bold enough. Pretend you're French. Channel your inner Jennifer Lawrence, when she wouldn't apologize after assholes stole her pictures. Tell them you like what you've got and that you'll flaunt it, baby." Suicidal if she could prove that I'd told her this, sure, but still true.

It's hard to attack the core identity of someone comfortable with themselves. High school students make easy targets for one another because no one is comfortable or willing to say, "Fuck you, this is who I am." They lack the intellectual tools to seriously question the society they make for themselves.

"Isn't that what sluts do?" Stacy said.

"If the word 'slut' ceased to be useful in American culture, such that it fell into disuse and eventually became a quaint marker of the early twenty-first century, the world would be a better place. Unfortunately, I don't see that happening in the short term."

"Me neither."

"Oh."

We paused. I let the conversation breathe, let Stacy work into what she was trying to get out.

"I just want a boyfriend!" she said.

If so, then, like many teenage girls, she had a curious way of going about finding one. "Stop using Arianna like a shield against romantic attention and go out and get one. How often do you have meaningful conversations with guys?"

Stacy gulped like I was quizzing her on the difference between Petrarchan and Shakespearean sonnets. "Like, sometimes?"

"Start there. Boyfriends usually start by talking. Go up and say hi. Smile. Ask what they like to do when they're not playing video games. Your job isn't to perform for men, unless you want to, but in this game girls make life needlessly hard on themselves. Boys do the same, of course, but so it goes."

"Oh."

"I mean, what about someone like Bill Wilson?"

"He's okay, I guess."

I liked Bill Wilson because he reminded me of myself: goofy, bright enough, too nervous—the kind of guy who'll grow into himself, take playing guitar to the next level, and do all right when he gets out of the local textbook loonybin.

"I'm not trying to lecture," I said, lecturing, "but you'll understand more when you get to college and take some human sexuality or sociology classes. Avoid most women's studies classes—they're overly political and obsessed with man-hating. The good ones are great, but the bad ones spread like fungus."

"You make college sound like it's paradise."

"It can be. It was for Melissa, for example—"

"How d'you know?"

I shifted, uncomfortable with what Stacy saw or intuited about me and her sister. I wanted to tell her that life is a series of disappointments punctuated by orgasms. But there's a limit to how much I or most teachers admit to students, which is why so many come to believe the world is an elaborate lie constructed by a conspiracy of adults. When full adults treat students like they're competent and capable, some of them resent the adult. Better for them to believe in *The Matrix* as a metaphor.

"We talk," I said. "We were friendly. You want a refill with regular coffee?"

"Sure."

The day's medium roast was an Ethiopian blend, its elaborate name written on the large chalkboard behind the counter. Laughter echoed from the other side of the room. Stumptown was a long narrow corridor, and Stacy and I were sitting near the windows. Where we could be seen. I told myself I wasn't hiding.

"I have to ask something I probably shouldn't," I said. "But I'm curious: why Sheldon, of all people? He was the cameraman, right?"

"I never said that to Principal Shorewell," Stacy said. She looked like she was about to scream or vomit, but she didn't. "I don't know."

"Haven't you asked yourself that?"

"Yeah," she said, too slowly, like she had a couple seconds' latency from reality. "I guess it was Sheldon because he asked."

"One other thing. Piece of advice. Try not to say or admit anything to anyone. Talk to your parents in private. Cops aren't usually there to help you; they're there to control you. To exert power over you. No matter their rhetoric or justifications."

"You mean Principal Shorewell?" Stacy said, all innocent.

"Use your imagination. I know you have one. That reminds me—you still want to take creative writing next year?"

"Yeah."

"Has your mom signed the permission slip?" I made the parents sign a form acknowledging that fiction often contains life's compelling elements, like sex, drugs, existentialism, and other real-life behaviors normally squelched by schools wary of lawsuits and parent complaints. The bedroom is literature's favorite playpen. No topic can or should be off-limit to novelists or philosophers.

If I'd been a smarter high school student, I would've spent less time worrying about forgettable tests and more time worrying about real projects and enjoying love, which is the real purpose of life anyway. The fiction I imagined myself writing would express that.

"Yeah," Stacy said.

"Great," I said.

I rose, she rose. She hugged me, which I wasn't expecting and didn't quite know what to do with.

"I can only give you advice," I said. "You have to walk the path. Let me also say this: what you're going through now seems like the end of the world. It isn't. It's temporary. High school is temporary."

"I get it," Stacy said. "It just seems like forever."

• • •

Sheldon

After the video came out and Arianna and Stacy got in trouble, I was walking by Stumptown on my way to get a sweet lid from a new shop that had opened next to Seattle University on Capitol Hill when I saw Mr. Sole and Stacy sitting there, right about to make the fuck out. Way too comfortable. So weird. Them sitting together said, man, something's a little bit up there. Something up in Mr. Sole's *pants.*

Marcus Stanislaw

I'm the school resource officer. That's another way of saying I bust heads when there's a problem. Most of the time, it's no bigs—guys wanting to show how tough they are in front of their girls, things like that. Passing weed at the bus stop. The tougher schools in south Seattle and the C-D have real problems. Least till the Amazonians drive them out.

This is a pretty cush job, for me and the teachers too. The students usually respect the badge to the face though they trash-talk behind the back and think it doesn't come back round. Everything comes back round. This job makes me believe in karma. The ones who get away over and over again are rarer than Vegas winners.

Laura called me to talk about the latest adventure in high school highs. I was among other things supposed to be the liaison with the District Attorney. She informed me of the facts and that the girls' families had been notified.

Teachers are supposed to inform the authorities whenever they suspect abuse of any kind, especially of a physical or sexual nature. Problem is, when the supposed abuser and abusee are the same person, who do you punish?

I told Laura what had been drilled into my own head, which was that we were supposed to check, given cases like these where parents will find out in a matter of time, about the incident. It's an awkward matter but must bear examination. I'd heard that it was not a bad thing to stop by the DA's office these days, and when I called I talked briefly with one of the assistant DAs. Young gal, not long out of law school from what I could tell. Good DAs want cases where people actually get hurt, not ones where teenagers take off their pants in poor taste and bad lighting.

The assistant DA's name was Kristen. She sounded cute, and when I told her about the situation over the telephone she followed the script at first.

"Have you seen the video in a professional capacity?" Kristen said.

"I have," I said. "Apart from the evidentiary copy the administrators have deleted it so far as I know." I didn't tell her about retaining a private evidentiary copy.

"Marcus, you see anything coercive?"

"No. Nothing obvious."

"Rapey?"

A stupid word, but I said, "They looked like they was having a fine time."

She laughed. "You'd know what that's like, huh?"

"I may have seen a woman having a fine time in my time."

"Okay, okay. You see any males?"

"No. If it wasn't a guy behind a camera, I've been dealing coke to Herbert seniors."

"Fair enough. Send me a copy. I may need to see the video in order for our office to make a final decision about pursuit in an issue such as this. Usually not worth it, but parents can make a real fuss."

"I see."

"Yes. One other question—did the individuals involved appear to be, uh, physically mature to you?"

"They did."

"That's good," she said.

"Should it matter?"

"The 'ick' factor. Legally, no, but…"

"But the law isn't everything."

"Right. Black-letter law responds to and creates social norm."

"Look at you, with the fancy school lawyer talk," I said.

"Too much school does that. Have you spoken with the young women involved?"

"Nah," I said. "They'd respond better to another female. You sound like you're equipped for the job." Like she'd got her own wardrobe of handcuffs whips and batons at home, for administration by a seasoned expert. "Delicate and tough at the same time. Meantime, the administration here'll handle it. I can, if you'd like to see about how these things can get out of control."

"A bit late now," Kristen said, like she'd know about such matters. "Already out of control."

"Yeah, yeah it is. These days you have to worry about the younger teachers as much as the students."

"Oh yeah? Tell me more," she said, suddenly interested. Prurient. Bad as the students themselves. People want to hear about dirty teenagers, and not just on the Internet.

"Look," I said, prepping a lie, "there's someone at the door. But a couple buddies are pretty proficient in salsa dancing. You should come out with us Thursday—that is, if you're available. Century Ballroom, on Capitol Hill."

She hesitated.

"We can arrange also for you to get that file," I said, regretting it as I did.

"I'd love to," she said.

Dundas Gekowski

I'm the assistant principal. My job is to be the guy people hate. I didn't set out to be the guy people hate, but when you're down in the bottom quarter of your class majoring in liberal arts with a minor in toking and wondering what you're going to do when you graduate, a couple easy education classes sounds pretty good, especially because they're filled with pretty girls. Well, girls.

A job appears and you take it. The first year is mentally tough but the hours are easy. You get older, you meet someone, you make someone, you start wondering how to make more money, you get the Masters from the mail—this is a long time ago—and the PhD in night school, you move up some, forgetting what you left behind—the person in the bottom third of their class who didn't have help from mom, let alone dad, and knew more than he knew anything that he needed a job. You still smile, you wonder if any of the kids who seem like they won't make it will make it, no matter what they look like.

I almost changed the name "Dundas" to "Dunstan" when a college girlfriend told that college boy about a character from a book. You can't really run away from yourself no matter how hard you try. Tell that to high school kids every week and they'll think you're an alien come to suck their blood.

Anyhow, after Laura got through talking to Arianna Stephenson and Stacy Leon, Laura came out and told me they wouldn't say who put them up to the video, no matter how she threatened. In a way I respected the decision. Showed character. Laura said she was going to call the parents and inform them of what had happened and asked me to apply some pressure.

I did. Neither would speak. I told them they'd been exploited, and they should have the guilty party made an example of. Neither would speak. Stacy was defiant from an intellectual standpoint, like she had principles and I wasn't going to shake them. Arianna seemed vacant, a hard girl to help, like she was not there, but off wherever her hair-twirling took her.

When I was in high school, I worked harder than any man alive to get girls nekkid, although I look back on it and wonder who that horndog was. He had an ancient Camaro, a big silver chain, props. All ways of saying, *Honey, what'cha doin' Friday?* And if they didn't have an answer, he'd have one for them. Most of them had an answer, but if ten said no and one said yes Friday was a success.

Now I understand why parents then and now try to get them to keep their damn clothes on and, when they do take them off, not to create evidence. Works as well as telling a grizzly not to eat the salmon. The younger teachers are just as bad. There was that one substitute, maybe 25, 26, who—hell, it doesn't matter. What matters is, they're just as bad, and the students get their ideas from them. It's an orgy these days, and I say this as someone who missed the 60s by a rat's tail. Got the druggie tail. Kids these days have no idea how good they have it. The white ones at least.

I told Arianna and Stacy they could be suspended. That wasn't entirely the case; when these matters happen outside of school hours, as they usually do, our hands are tied beyond notifying parents. Hell, I just got through an article that went through the Washington administrator mailing list that starts, "Indiana school district violated the First Amendment rights of two teenage girls who were punished for posting sexually suggestive photos on MySpace during their summer vacation, a federal judge ruled."

Stacy said that I could take it up with her family's lawyer. I was caught trying to remember: *was* her father a lawyer? Did he work for a law firm? I'd love to think the threat a bluff but it's hard to tell. It wasn't long after that her mother arrived, told Stacy to shut up, and said they were leaving. I wouldn't want to be that girl, facing an angry older female. I also didn't get why she didn't crack. They almost all do, even the superficially tough ones. Something about her was different.

Scott Sole

Arianna was sullen and unhappy when I got to her. The contrast with Stacy was so sharp that I wondered how the two became friends or frenemies. She wouldn't communicate. Help as much as you can, but sometimes the patient says no and you have to watch them walk out of the emergency room, and the best you can do is monitor the closing doors behind them, hoping they aren't going to find themselves back in your office with a problem ten times worse days or weeks or months or years later.

I gave up, wished her the best, and moved on.

• • •

Stacy Leon

It hurt bad, but I did it. I turned off my Facebook like Mr. Sole suggested. Without it, I was so bored. I spent two full days at home—part of my suspension—and barely talked. Mr. Sole says that the ability to be alone and think, without distractions, is an essential and endangered skill in the modern world. Those are the kinds of words he uses. Most people roll their eyes or stare into space when he talks that way, but I wonder if he's right. He says shit he qualifies with, "You might understand this when you're older," like he's daring us to understand it or pretend to understand it now.

My parents yelled at me. Oh, they yelled. I cowered. They told me I was never going to leave the house again if I didn't tell them who was behind the camera. Eventually, they came to admire me for not giving away my friend, or whatever Sheldon was. A friend, I guess, but the worst friend ever.

I dreaded going back to school with what I later realized must be the same feeling Hester had, going up on that scaffold with her baby.

Scott Sole

I never asked Stacy or Arianna more about why they did what they did. The possible reasons were obvious. For thrills; they liked the attention; fame; to appear sexy; to seduce; to test their powers; the excitement that comes from violating taboos; to perform; someone or more than one person asked them; because it aroused them; because they wanted to do it. Those were all, in some way, facets of the same unnameable reason, which we might call "desire," but even that's inadequate. Lots of things don't have a reason we can name. Five seconds before you get off, what is there to say, really, about how you feel, about all the leading up to and all that will come after?

The other possibility was coercion. I saw the video. I have admittedly seen many in its genre, but those were impersonal and online. If they were coerced, Arianna and Stacy did a pro job of hiding it. When we do something we want to deny, we often blame someone else after. But the blame is just that. The real culprit lies within.

Sheldon

The Leadership crew runs the assemblies, which happen the last Friday of each month. In assemblies sports teams do their thing, strutting while they're supposed to be about school spirit and shit like that. If I can get a girl, I skip the assemblies and, you know.

That Friday after the tape got out I tried to get Arianna to skip with me, but she wouldn't. It was her first day back, post-suspension. We'd gone straight to awkward. She blamed me but not enough to tell me to fuck off.

So I was sitting with the sophomores, Roger near me, Stacy too, when the soccer team came out to kick the ball around. The robotics club showed this cool spider thing that's awesome and freaks the shit out of the girls. If the damn thing was big as a car, it'd be real scary.

I'm yawning, ready for a nap, when the lights go down for a video. Three AV guys do the projectors, the music. We're stuck in this big ugly gym, so we can't hear for shit. The robotics guys are all excited because the video's about their competition. Virgins who might rule the world eventually. Maybe I should join. Couldn't be worse than most of the shit I do after school.

I close my eyes and wait for it to end, and am kind of dozing on the bleacher when I hear people start gasping and laughing.

Scott Sole

Lola Messina and I were outside the gym in a light drizzle. It smelled like moss and teen spirit. Assemblies are almost always the same, with the goal of raising supposed school spirit—along with the status of athletes through adulation. Most of the students waited only for their friends to be recognized, or for bloopers: would someone fall down? A Leadership kid go off her marks, with the suspension that was sure to follow? It's like a car race without a winner, everyone waiting for the crash that comes too infrequently to make it interesting.

Lola and I got along because she shared my taste for gossip and scandal, especially the kind we, as teachers, shouldn't be talking about. She may also have shared my taste for women but we rarely discussed south-of-the-border matters *that* explicitly, and I knew vaguely of her besties-with-benefits experiences. She was telling me about how she was tired of hookups and ready to get married, since she was 32 and her eggs wouldn't last forever, and I was telling her about Lori Gottlieb's book *Marry Him!*

"We should be smoking," Lola said. "Everyone who skipped assemblies at my school went down to the creek to smoke."

"I don't smoke," I said. "A little green now and then."

"Neither do I, except when I'm drunk. How's busty Sabrina, by the way?"

Before I could answer evasively about this woman I met on the street using day game, we heard the startle inside. Two double doors were open. I popped my head in first. The gym was dark except for the footage being projected on a wall: I recognized a flash of flesh, then someone pulled the projector's power, but it wasn't so easy to erase the memory of all 1,500 Herbert students, of Stacy and Arianna's bare breasts.

"What the fuck was that?" Lola said.

"Someone's idea of a joke," I said. "Like life."

Arianna Stephenson

I was so over the assemblies it's not even funny. If I have to go to this school for another two years, I'm going to go fucking crazy. I used to look at those girls who cut themselves and think, "They're totally crazy." Now I look at them and think, maybe they're the only sane ones.

Scott Sole

Someone cut the power, but the power of the video buzzed the school like a saw. Dundas tried to retake control by shouting, "People, people, settle down." The teachers were standing, waving their arms like they were directing planes, or folding them, stern like drill sergeants. Neither strategy was especially effective. As the mob found where Stacy sat, she stood up.

Her mouth was set. I'd never seen anyone so profoundly solemn, but she put one foot in front of the other, raised her hands, and took a deep bow. A ballerina's bow, though she was still stonefaced. A few people laughed, but something about her dignity caught the attention of everyone in that building. I was riveted, and I was supposed to be; the entire school began clapping for her, but it was a clap cleansed of the sarcasm and irony high school students don like armor. If she'd done anything else she'd have made herself a target, but sometime between Friday and the Tuesday I saw the tape, she'd gained some sense of inner resolve that in another culture would've marked her transition into the adult world.

When she rose from her bow, hands sweeping wide around her body, she put a tentative foot on the bleacher in front of her. The other students parted. Had she taken ballet as a child? If so, she'd never mentioned it, but only training could explain her extraordinary grace as she descended, her head up the entire time like she didn't need to know where she was going. Truth is so hard, mockery so easy. She either didn't have or didn't take her backpack; it was like she was floating free of all the burdens that lock most of us so securely to the earth.

The room hushed as she walked across the narrow side of the gym, underneath the gleaming basketball backboard. She came straight towards me, and for some absurd reason I imagined she was going to leap into my arms and kiss me. You see someone else's moment and think you're a part of it. No one tried to stop Stacy's progress. I doubt she even saw me as she glided out, momentarily transformed into the princess of a fairy tale, with all the grace and dignity she didn't display on the tawdry tape, beautiful and remote as the moon. If it was performance, it was extraordinary. But I didn't think it was performance: it was need transformed into a feeling so pure it couldn't be named.

Dundas Gekowski

Every so often, you get one of those students who breaks the rule with such aplomb that you can't really punish them. That's what I saw with Stacy Leon. One time, when I was still teaching math, this guy walks in ten minutes late, holding a takeout sandwich and a drink. Because of the placement of the door, he's got to walk straight past me, hook a left, and sit in the first cluster of seats.

He's looking at me the whole time he's walking to his seat and tips his food to me like he's saying hi as he walks past, two buds passing on the sidewalk. I'm about to chew him out, but there's something so cool I don't do it.

Of course, he tries the same thing two weeks later, and I have to lecture him and the class on how the joke is only funny the first time, not the second, and you can get away with something once that'll never fly twice. It's a teachable moment. He shows up to class on time the rest of the semester. I don't have to go all disciplinarian on his ass.

Yeah. That's what I saw Stacy Leon do, except I didn't think she had it. I didn't peg her as the kind to make adult cinema for a boy or as a means of self-expression, either, but if teaching teaches you anything it should be to expect the unexpected and that character is more fluid than you think.

• • •

Laura Shorewell

I interrogated Ronald Chen, Frank Malone, and Jon Gibson about the pornography shown at the spring spirit assembly. All were members of Leadership, who were charged with setting the video, and Jon was the member of the robotics club who made the video for the spirit assembly and who was charged with splicing the forbidden footage. All swore they'd not tampered with the actual video. Someone was lying.

Dundas Gekowski said he'd reviewed the video the evening before, when Leadership students were preparing. It showed students writing code, the mechanical spider being built, and the spider crawling over minor obstacles. It was a technical triumph of the sort too rarely celebrated in high schools, whose members believe that the only thing that matters in life is the placing of balls in the right receptacles in order to score points in a predefined time limit.

I asked how many students had access to the video-editing station over the course of the evening, and he said he didn't know. All of them said they didn't know. What they didn't know could fill the universe.

From what I understand, virtually everyone at the school has received the video one way or another. At the time, I had been the principal of Herbert for four years; I've been told at conferences that schools were much easier to manage in the age before "smart" phones that enable dumb behavior. At the start of each year we have assemblies on the dangers of disseminating nude photos. Said assemblies are as effective as telling horny baboons not to fornicate or fling their feces. We have awareness weeks. We have handouts.

The photos fly anyway. Porn has become modern sex ed. They're fools, but they don't think about it in the moment. There's also the little problem: what's sexier than saying, *I trust you enough not to send these to anyone?* I'm not so old I can't get it.

Roger, Frank, and Jon denied editing the film with such vehemence that I wanted to believe them. Students will lie with the fervency of religious converts to get out of trouble. They're a lot like adults in that respect. I wanted to believe them, but someone also needed to be punished. For the sake of the group, and for appearance. Not knowing what else to do, I suspended each of them for a day for failing to double-check their work and maintain appropriate physical access to their computers. The entire school technically committed a felony, which may say more about legal stupidity than it does about anything else, but the fact remains.

As for the video situation, frankly, I didn't know who to blame, but I was vaguely suspicious of Scott Sole's role. When there's a sexting scandal, he's too often standing by the side of whoever's involved. Whose side is he on: ours, or theirs?

Scott Sole

The girls weren't formally punished more than they'd already been. Social punishment was a different matter. The fallout from other girls was probably cruelest. Many are little Saurons. When guys whisper or shout propositions in the hallway, they're perceived as simply being guys. When girls turn their backs as a group—which I saw one bunch do, days later, as Stacy walked by—they're trying to ostracize a girl by taking away feminine social power. On some level it didn't matter who put up the video: anyone could've and the damage was done.

Each high school student is utterly enraptured in their own false drama; if they could only realize that others are suffering or will suffer in the same way, high school would be more human. It wouldn't be a contemporary American high school anymore, either. Might be a good thing, but I saw it as pretty unlikely.

Arianna Stephenson

My parents grounded me for a month. They were all like, I can't understand why you'd do this to us, like it had anything to do with them. It didn't. It has everything to do with me. They went on and on about how people would think I came from a bad home, how they'd think I'd been abused when I was a kid. If they think that, they're stupid. I mean, you can come from anywhere and still want to, you know. You know? I bet so.

Guys like Bill Wilson kept trying to be nice to me. I didn't really want their sympathy. Barrett Rodriguez kept inviting me to go out on his boat with some "guys" to have a party. From the way he'd look at me, I knew what he meant, and I wasn't having any part of that. I was grounded. My parents decided I should get some therapy too. Like, so I could talk. When I shouted at them that I was allowed to want to get some, like everyone else, they shouted back that I wasn't allowed to have sex. Yeah, good luck. Bit late. They forget how much James's friends liked to sleep over, before he went to college? I haven't.

• • •

Stacy Leon

I didn't go to school for another three days after the assembly. Scott texted, "People can transcend themselves and their place if they want to bad enough." I wrote back asking how, but he didn't reply. I sort of got what he meant. It didn't make the nastiness any easier, but I remembered something else he'd told me: some things must be endured until they pass.

My parents had to talk to a lawyer, who said that prosecutors were unlikely to press charges over a homemade video that'd only made it to school because of someone else's actions.

Arianna Stephenson

My parents got me a therapist to work through "issues" related to my "behavior" and "acting out." She was this old woman who'd get me to sit down on this fat leather chair in her office and talk to me for like an hour. I'd rather have been watching TV.

I was supposed to see her twice a week at first. I told her all kinds of stuff about dreams, but not the dirty parts, and my life. She'd ask about the dirty parts and promise that it wasn't her job to judge—it was only her job to listen. Yeah, right, and actresses don't get fake boobs.

It was hard to explain what was going on to anyone, like my dumb friends, and how a lot of girls wouldn't talk to me because I was That Girl.

"Do you have any artistic hobbies?" she asked.

"What d'you mean?"

"Art can be a means of expressing yourself. Making music, taking photos, writing, or painting—none of those activities necessarily depend on people around you, and therefore can be a means of filtering and shaping experience in a way that makes it meaningful for you, the artist, and others who experience your work. Art cultivates an independent mind and spirit that is robust against the attacks of others in the social world."

"Woah," I said.

"My point is that you might consider finding some way of focusing your energy and aggression that doesn't require a man's gaze to give it meaning. Art can be one avenue, though it isn't the only one. I want you to try reading a book called *My Name is Asher Lev*. I'll bring a copy to our next session. Many teenagers feel a sense of ennui—of meaninglessness, I mean—because our society isn't set up to offer challenges commensurate with their skills."

"I don't, like, understand half of that. You use big words."

"I do, sometimes. As you learn big words, the possible range of the ideas you can express increases."

"You sound like my English teacher."

"He's a smart man, then, and you should listen to him. Great teachers are rare and powerful. They can reveal things about yourself to yourself, and about your relationship to the world that would take you years to find on your own, if you ever did. Self-discovery is never complete."

"Okay."

"Self-expression is often soothing." I'd heard that music soothes the savage beast, and for a moment I imagined my therapist as a tiger or an armadillo. "Have you ever played or wanted to play an instrument?"

"No."

"How about paint or draw?"

"Not really. I doodle in class sometimes." Doodle dicks. I can be such a fucking guy.

"What about write? Fiction, stories, that kind of thing. Many people your age write online now."

"Kind of, I guess. I mean, there's a creative writing class that Mr. Sole, the English teacher who uses big words, teaches."

"Many people start creative writing by writing variations on the stories generated by their everyday lives. One could argue a major novelist like Philip Roth does."

"Okay, yeah. I mean, like I said, I could try to get into this class. Mr. Sole's class. He was nice to me after the thing happened at the assembly."

"That might be good for you," she said. "But you don't have to take a class to write. Writing is open to anyone with paper or a computer."

"Yeah, but, I mean—if I don't, you know, take a class, how will I know if I'm doing it right?"

"For you, right now, it's not about right and wrong. It's about finding an outlet for your frustrations in a safe environment, rather than experimenting with actions that may have negative consequences down the line."

"I'm not frustrated."

"Your acting out indicates otherwise."

"I wasn't acting out. I, you know, liked it, kind of. Not what the girls did to me after, but, you know, it's kind of fun, being a star."

"Okay. That's the kind of thing you might wish to explore through a skill-based field, then. I see what you mean. Perhaps you should try to get in this class. It may calm you and make you happier. So you don't need to act out."

"Yeah," I said. "Let me, like, try tomorrow."

• • •

Scott Sole

I was getting towards the end of that year, my fourth, and pretty happy for it. Melissa talked about returning to Herbert a student teacher. I had a sweet girl on hand, who ultimately turned out to be somewhat boring intellectually while being enormously sexually compatible. The only thing that really bothered me was a sense that my opportunities for change were drifting out of focus, like a zoom suffering lens creep.

It was a vague sense of discontent, not entirely articulated, of closing opportunity windows. Like the military and other government work that became sclerotic decades ago, the longer a teacher stays teaching, the better off they are staying longer. After 30 years, teachers in Seattle get 60% of their final salary and sweet health benefits, for life. By the time I would get to the shockingly advanced age of 52, those benefits will have been budgeted out of existence by the wave of teachers retiring before me. But something like it would probably remain.

Which meant that, if I didn't make a change soon, an increasing salary and closing proximity on the magic 30-year mark would make a real career change increasingly unlikely. I'd have to settle for having local effects on students who might go on to do important work, instead of doing important work myself.

In the short term, life was good, but I have a bad habit of thinking out further than I should. The two temperaments were dueling within me the afternoon, about three weeks before school finished, that Arianna walked in my door after school.

• • •

Arianna Stephenson

Mr. Sole is one of those teachers who encourages you to talk to him. Most teachers want you to go somewhere else so they don't have to look at you, but he's different. I *thought* he was different, until I tried to turn in my application for the creative writing class. I threw together a story about a girl who really feels and is waiting at this bus stop when a guy walks by. I wrote it fast but good. Plus, Mr. Sole knew me from being on the newspaper. He really liked my work!

"Hey," I said to Mr. Sole.

"Hey, Arianna," he said. "How's it going?"

"Kind of okay." I got kind of seated next to him. He had all these books on shelves behind him, like he was trying to intimidate me by saying, "I've done all this reading and you haven't." There're so many colors on the wall.

"What's the matter?"

"I—um—it's been a tough year."

"Tell me about it."

"Yeah. The video thing. I had a kind of a question for you."

"Yes?"

"Can I sign up for, you know, your creative writing class next semester?"

"Schedules have already been assigned—it may be too late."

"I bet I can get permission from Principal Shorewell. I've been working on, like, a story." It was kind of a lie. The kind he wanted to hear. So I told it to him. Teachers like it when you tell them what they want to hear. Like boys. I like boys.

"What about?"

"A girl who—you know, some bad things happen to her in high school."

"Based on real-life events?"

"Kinda."

"And you've not got a blog or Tumblr or whatever the cool new tool may be?"

"I mean…" I said. He didn't need to know about that. "It's, like, therapy."

"Therapy?"

"My therapist suggested I take this class. That I write. It's important for my recovery"

"You have a note from her?"

"I can get one."

"Look, I'm not a therapist," Mr. Sole said. "If you want therapy, delivered via words, read Nietzsche. I'm just a teacher. If your therapist wants to do some kind of treatment with writing, it's up to him or her to supervise it."

"Oh," I said. "Wouldn't this be, like, creative?"

He sighed, like he was tired of me. I was tired of him and wanted to leave. Not as bad as I wanted him to say yes.

"Even creative writing is a misnomer," he said. "I mean, does writing about stuff that's made up automatically make you more creative than writing about facts or ideas? Of course not. But we got this stupid name, and now we're stuck with it. I'd rather call the class 'fiction writing' because that would be more accurate and less pretentious."

"Pretentious?" Weird word.

"Yeah, like, snooty. Looking down its nose at you. You know what I mean?"

"I know exactly what you mean. But I—I thought you'd give me a chance." And not be a jerk, like every guy I'd ever met.

"Look," Scott said. Teachers can be worn down. "Bring me a sample tomorrow. Getting into creative writing is like varsity soccer: you have to try out. Pretty much anyone can make frosh/soph, which is what basic English classes are like, but if you want to play in the big leagues, you better have the footwork. There are plenty of classes that you can get by showing up. This ain't one."

"Uh, okay," I said.

"You see what I'm doing there? With the metaphor? You know, the footwork is like your ability to wield metaphors?"

"Yeah, I mean, I get it."

Scott Sole

"Recovery?" What was she talking about?

There was something unsettling about the basic insincerity of Arianna, what she said, how she said it, and what she did. It didn't seem a trick or a conscious behavior on her part: it was who she was. She lived in the eternal present. I was tempted to ask Laura and Dundas, who made up the schedules, to keep her out of my classes, but that would only draw needless suspicion and curiosity: why *her*? Teachers rarely actively exclude students.

Arianna reminded me of an Arizona State University freshman named Elizabeth Hawkenson, who I'd read about when she made the blog rounds for appearing in a porn and holding up her school ID. College students watch too much porn. When the news first surfaced, she proclaimed that she'd never do something like that because she "had morals." She wasn't willing or able to articulate the idea that doing porn wasn't immoral, and she apparently didn't consider that video evidence would be easily found. An appeal to vague "morals" was enough of a reason to shut down the conversation. The smarter porn stars are loudly proud, proclaiming that they like to get laid and don't care who knows it.

Student personalities do suddenly shift, but I didn't see Arianna as the kind of girl to have epiphanies, or to have much going on inside. I'd met bad news girls in bars and parties and online and knew them well enough to avoid them for anything beyond base pleasure. Guys with experience know girls who make trouble by accident—by not paying attention—and that quality was yoked to low-grade ambition. But ambition for what? I couldn't really answer the question for Arianna. I wouldn't be surprised to see Arianna on the cover of *US Weekly* one day.

Women know the male equivalent of Arianna, who tend to be debauched players ready to rock 'em and leave 'em. Lola Messina had had a few of those, but Lola was also intellectually honest enough to say that she wanted base pleasure, enjoyed base pleasure, and wasn't going to apologize for base pleasure.

I told Lola about Arianna and Stacy that day at happy hour in Capitol Hill with Lola's friends, who liked hearing her speak French, because the language itself sounded dirty even when she said things like, "Pass me the olives" or "I need to catch the next bus so I'm not stranded downtown." Though I doubted they'd admit as much, Lola's friends liked the vicarious thrill of high school gossip—perhaps because high school has the largest gap of any life period between actions or beliefs *seeming* important versus *being* important.

Lola had plenty of experience—too much, but she was cute so I understood—with student crushes of the sort any attractive woman will inspire in teenage boys. One day all those teenage boys will become equally helpless adult men.

"Scott," Lola said after I told her about the creative writing incident. "Arianna's a 16-year-old girl. Of course she's conniving."

"It's in a way that's destructive," I said.

"Don't overreact. She'll be okay. She's not another Heather Karr."

"I worry," I said. "It only takes one unstable girl…"

"Heather Karr?" one of the friends said.

"Senior girl with a drug problem from two years ago," Lola said.

"Yeah," I said. "She apparently sold out a couple guys from her class when she got busted. It was ugly."

"Correct," Lola said. "The real thing is, why are you risking so much by talking to Arianna? Or to Stacy?"

There were lies I could tell because the truth, that I was trying to help, seemed improbable. What to do when the truth seems a lie? Instead I said, "They don't seem guilty of anything more than flashing out momentarily against the moral gloom of the stupid world they live in."

"Scott, this isn't Pakistan. Proportion counts. Also: Moral? A word you've never said before."

"Because it doesn't mean much. It applies here in a very negative sense. If I don't tell them, who will?"

Another friend, this one a guy who wanted to be the center of attention, said everyone was going to need another round. He was the sort whose idea of deep conversation involved analysis of why the team from one geographic region defeated the team from another geographic region in the major contest last weekend.

"They'll figure it out for themselves," Lola said.

"Why not be a catalyst?" I said. "Most of them can be helped. I just want to avoid the ones who're gonna melt down—or conventionally explode."

"So Scott. Who's the latest woman in your life?"

"Oh," I said. "No one. Girl I met on the bus. Not bad in the *fesses*, but, well… Not sure up here," I said, tapping my head, but I was still thinking about Arianna. It's a bad sign when I can't get them out of my head, turn it off at the end of the day, refocus on art.

Arianna Stephenson

I meant to write a story or something, I really did, but it was just so hard. To sit there, at the computer, and, like, think of something. I'd get home, and there'd be something on, and I'd need to listen to the music to get in the right mood, and then Stacy and Sheldon would come over to hang out, and then I'd need to do, you know, my stupid math homework. Stacy wanted to tell me about her crushes, Sheldon wanted to talk about the band he'd heard, Icy Death Spike or The Big Pussies.

My therapist kept telling me I could show her my writing if I needed to, but really, what's the point? It's practically as pointless as writing for the newspaper. Totally dumb. I'm too smart for this stuff.

• • •

Scott Sole

Teaching creative writing classes to high schoolers is usually futile, like performing CPR on the dead. Most of them—students, I mean, not the dead—don't even know themselves, let alone anyone else. "Creativity," even un-reinforced by knowledge, is somehow taken as a virtue, a magical elixir that will fix problems from the individual to societal level. *Creative* writing, however horribly executed, must be good, unlike that dull, stilted writing in complete sentences demanded by boring English teachers who still somehow think Shakespeare is important.

People like Arianna or her half-wit therapist, if the therapist exists, assume writing fiction will be easy. From what I knew of other schools and teachers, creative writing classes usually were, and had the nutritional value of a McDonald's "Value" Meal. But I was trying to impart something real, which is challenging and dangerous, especially when it comes to art. Art is dark. It expresses the darkness felt in every soul. Schools prefer their art to be safely dead—yanked out of the water, whacked over the head with a club, gutted, and put on ice. Live art pushes whatever boundaries we've communally put up at the time. In that respect it's dangerous, but art is also the way we work through the traumas we wish we didn't have. Despite canonization, parents won't accept their son or daughter writing the next *Lolita*.

Or accept their child's teacher writing the next *Lolita*. Sometimes I've wondered what would happen if some publisher picked up *She Wasn't That Into Me*, a novel in the McInerney style about 20-somethings' sex lives and bed hopping. It was my third effort and still uncompleted, but one day I knew it would be completed. It was preceded by a navel-gazing adolescent novel that I now shudder to think I wrote and a science fiction gore and sex fest that was really about what happened when Lily Grossman dumped me junior year. Emotions were rawer then. I hadn't accepted the cruelty of the game of life and evolution. Sexual frustration is the foundation of plenty of art. In schools, ambition and pretense often trump substance.

The good English teachers have chapter one, and maybe more than chapter one, sitting in the proverbial drawer— that is to say, a modern hard drive. They had and have the ambition to start. The bad ones never even had that. You can see the same thing among students: the better ones have the ambition. The Italians have a saying: "*Chi ben comincia è a metà dell'opera*"—a good start is the halfway mark of any good work.

When I knew I'd say "no" to Arianna, I worried that I'd be perceived as playing favorites, which was probably better than being perceived as covering my ass from all manner of problems Stephenson related. Fortunately, she never came back to follow up.

Arianna Stephenson

A couple days after I asked Scott to be in his class, I realized I wasn't going to be able to write the story in time. I was *so* busy. Adults don't understand. Instead I went to see Principal Shorewell to tell her about the situation and see if she could get me in.

I got to her office and kind of told Principal Shorewell that Scott said I could be in his class. She really understood how hard it had been for me lately, because she said, "Oh, okay," and took me out of Weight Training and right into his class. She didn't call him or anything. I was so nervous walking in that I thought I was going to die, but it wasn't a big deal. Which makes sense. I mean, why would it be?

• • •

Scott Sole

Partway through that summer—the summer before Melissa came back—I got an email about finalizing class schedules. Since journalism and creative writing require permission to enter, I checked those first.

Creative writing had one mistake: Arianna Stephenson was on the roster, and I very specifically remembered her *not* giving me a story or any other kind of writing that indicated some very basic level of background reading that would make creative writing somewhat useful for her. You'd be surprised by how many people say they never read books but want to write them. I mean, do composers run into people who say, "I don't like or listen to music, but I want to write a symphony?" But there are all these people—and not just high school students—who are so far from having the foundation writing and reading skills that hearing them talk about wanting to write anything for anyone other than themselves is laughable.

Arianna was in my normal English class too, and that I couldn't help.

Email is dangerous because of the traces it leaves. I called Laura and heard her tell me how she thought Arianna had permission, and I told her that, quite the contrary, not only had I not given Arianna permission, but she'd not turned in a writing sample or a permission slip signed by her parents. I didn't need an emotionally erratic liar in the class, despite the wide overlap between "emotionally erratic liars" and "writers."

Laura hadn't double checked with me because she's a principal with many real problems beyond a marginally mendacious girl working the bureaucracy, and I admitted to myself what I wouldn't out loud: I admired Arianna for her cleverness.

"I see," Laura said. "Want to call her and discuss the matter with her? Or should I?"

"I don't think that's necessary," I said. "She had her chance, and she didn't take it, and she evidently created some kind of misunderstanding between the two of you. Can you find another class for her?"

"During that time slot, there's a mythology class Lola is teaching, and AP Microeconomics with Dustin Wolfe. She was in P.E., but that's full now."

"I see her happier in mythology." Which is easier than any class that uses math.

"You're sure you don't want to consult with her?"

"I don't see any need to," I said. "None at all."

Arianna Stephenson

On the first day of school my junior year, we had to pick up our schedules. On paper. Fucking stone age. I was with Stacy, and we were laughing over some of the dumb things the freshmen were wearing. It's like, do they look in the mirror before they come to school?

My first class was math, and I was pretty much ready to see if I could see anyone new. Ronald Chen distracted me when he was like, "Hey Arianna, have you been to the movies lately?" I suggested he go fuck himself because no one else would.

There was this class—mythology, what?—that I didn't want. I double checked my schedule and saw creative writing wasn't on it. He'd fucked me. Stacy and Sheldon got whatever they wanted, whenever they wanted. Was I not pretty enough or something? Not pretty enough, like Melissa, or something, or someone else? But I was thinner than Melissa. Not thin enough, I guess.

I was in his regular English class but didn't bring it up then. After school I hoped I could still somehow get into creative writing. It was supposed to be cake. Stacy said everyone got an A, commas or none or whatever. Mr. Sole was big on commas. Loser.

His door was shut, and when I came in he acted like I was radioactive poison or something. He pushed a few papers away and scooted to the far side of his desk, keeping it between us.

"You wanna prop it open?" he said.

"What?" I said.

"The door."

I sat across from him, in the yellow plastic chair shaped like an egg, so your hips never fit right. Designed for boys like everything else. Mr. Sole looked at me. I looked at him. I tried to be sultry, kind of, or pretty.

"What's on your mind?" Mr. Sole said. "I'm sorry—I should say, how was your summer?"

"Pretty good," I said, thinking of how my brother's friend Ben had come back from Whitman in a really good mood, and how pissed my brother had been when he found out that stuff. Like he hadn't tried for Stacy.

I went on, "I, you know, signed up for your creative writing class, but I don't have it on my schedule."

Mr. Sole seemed very far away. Sheldon gave that feeling to me sometimes. I was uncomfortable. To break up the quiet I passed Mr. Sole a copy of my schedule. Instead of his class during third period, I was in Spanish, then pre-calc, then mythology, then weight training, then AP Government. High school is bullshit.

He kept not saying anything.

"Why, uh, didn't I get in creative writing?" I said. "Stacy got in."

"There were far more applicants than places," he said. "Yours was very strong, but it was a very competitive year."

"Is this about that—other thing?"

"I'm not sure what you're talking about, but no."

"Then why didn't I get a place?"

"Simple: too many people and too few spots. I'm sorry. You didn't give me a writing sample or return your parental permission slip. If there were fewer applicants, you'd be in. Like soccer, there are only so many positions on the field—"

"You said that to me already."

"Oh. At this point there's nothing I can do. Maybe second semester—work on your writing and reading this semester. Art is a lifelong project. Show me what you've done at the end of the semester and we'll talk."

He wanted to get rid of me. He hated me.

It wasn't what he said that really bothered me. It was the lying. He didn't like me. He was afraid of me, like a little girl. No one thinks about how teachers can hate too. It was so weird that a teacher hated me so much that he wouldn't let me into class. Stacy never had those problems. I bet Stacy had done everything she needed to do to get in.

So why didn't I? Why did I have to take hard, stupid classes like Spanish?

Much later—the next semester—I saw him with Melissa, the slut, and I got to thinking how he's not the only person who can lie when he needs to.

PART IV

Laura Shorewell

The principal of a school is fundamentally caught among three forces: the school board, parents, and teachers, none under the principal's control. The school board wants the principal to improve test scores above all. Parents want their kids to get As, or at least not have to try very hard. What happens to the other students is immaterial. Teachers—or, more specifically, their unions—want to make sure principals can't fire anyone.

If you can think, you probably know that these are mutually incompatible goals. Unions have largely succeeded. The principal's hands are tied, and she has to use persuasion as much as she can. There are limits to persuasion if the persuader doesn't have a big stick in her hand. The school board wants glowing test scores, Ivy League college admissions, and a steady stream of accomplishments lovingly described in public venues. The goal of the board conflicts heavily with the goals of teachers and students, and the principal doesn't real suck with any of these groups. Give me the chance to hire and fire teachers at will and I might accomplish something.

At first I didn't see the Scott Sole dirty blog post was a problem: an anonymous note with a URL isn't a basis for anything about anything. Free speech, blah blah blah. The note said I should see it and was unsigned. Judging by the low quality of the paper, it had come from a library print-out, which pointed to a student. The lack of capital letters or standard punctuation further pointed to a student, or to one of the longer-serving and less literate teachers.

I thought about all that later, of course, when I tried to decide who would have a reason to dislike Scott. He could be smarmy and annoying but didn't seem to collect overt enemies. At the time, life intervened. Dundas caught a party kid selling Molly via a phone app developed by the budding entrepreneur himself. The note at my desk marinated next to a couple catalogues of dubious teaching supplies that were supposed to revolutionize the learning experience in proportion to the amount of money a district was willing to waste.

Drugs were always exciting, considering my Mary Karr-esque history with them. Eventually I got back round to the blog stuff. Today, most teachers applying for jobs are smart enough to set their social media profiles to private, so I can't read them. The dumb ones don't privatize. They don't pass the mirror test—someone holds a mirror up to your mouth; if it fogs, pass.

Look, I don't personally care if you had to strip your way through college, or whatever, hell I might admire you for it, but if you make a point of making a point of it, I've got no choice but to respond. Otherwise it's my ass next. Things I did in college stayed in college where they belong. When

I got back to the public page, it had fallen below some of Scott's ramblings about books, but it was still there: Scott apparently wanted everyone with an Internet connection to see some girl's slick backside.

People are funny about schools. It was time to have a chat.

Scott Sole

I knocked on Laura the lion's door, no whip or chair in hand. Laura told me to come in. Her mouth was a hyphen. Laura was young enough that you could still imagine her as a girl. No wonder Dundas was crazed, having to be a vice principal while the top job went to someone two decades his junior. For Dundas, I don't think being passed over was a money thing. It was a respect thing. As in, he got none. No assistant principal does.

It's not like it took a great deal of umph to be a principal. Principals took shit from parents, students, the unions, the media, the mayor: An exigent principal can't exist. Dundas had been an administrator long enough to become a shit-taking expert.

That day I sensed that I was going to get no respect, though I wondered if Laura had learned about the sandwich with me between my student teacher and a girl. Laura had those library glasses on, with the square tops and rounded bottoms, a beaded thread going around her head. Could be sexy in the right circumstances.

She scooted those glasses to the end of her nose, like she couldn't believe what she was seeing.

"Scott," she said. "I'd ask about your weekend, but I'd rather cut to the chase. What's with the crap you're putting on the Internet?"

"Pardon?" I said. Had she found the Reddit Gone Wild posts? The drunken Pornhub video with a former stripper? Those didn't have my face in them and I didn't have any tattoos students were likely to have seen.

"Your blog?" she said.

"The essay about *The Scarlet Letter*? I thought it synthesized the way literature affects life and life affects literature quite well, along with important approaches to teaching, and—"

"Yeah, yeah, I mean the—" she fluttered her hands, searching for words "—spanking post. Christ." She swiveled her monitor to show me the post, complete with pictures. No nipples. No genitals. I was mostly in the clear. It was education. Art, even. Right?

"I don't think it's about s- spanking—it's mostly about, uh, construction, or something," I said. Good thing she hadn't found the post about sex wedge pillows: ideal for angling your female partner for maximum pleasure, or so Babeland's marketing material proclaimed. "Although other activities could, uh, also be performed as needed."

"Yes, that's wonderful, pumpkin. Take it down."

"Who told you about it?" I said.

"I read all my teachers' intellectual production."

I cocked my head, faux wounded and curious. The only intellectual production most teachers emit could be eliminated entirely via the judicious use of Beano or Gas-X.

"Don't you think," she said, as if talking to a daft student, "this will compromise your effectiveness as a teacher?"

"I don't see why," I said, like this was a philosophy seminar instead of a high school.

"Tell me at least that this person isn't the person I think this person is."

"She isn't." How could Laura know Kate? That made no sense.

"Good, because I'm going to talk to her. For now, delete this crap." Laura gestured vaguely but playfully to her computer. "From now on I'm also keeping an extra close eye on your work online."

"You're not going to tell me who finked?"

"You don't want to know. Knowledge isn't always good. Assume my eyes are everywhere. Take the damn thing down, will you?"

I liked her sparkle, liked how she was handling the situation. Wasn't going to be confrontational if she could avoid it. She'd make a great warden.

"If I don't?"

"We're going to strap you to that thing and do what we need to convince you of the error of your ways. Like a gangster movie, but with less blood. You want to be like that guy from *The Departed*?"

"Which one?"

"The one who ends up dead at the end."

"Doesn't he get that actress? The cute one?"

"Vera Farmiga. Take it down, Scott. Make things easy on yourself. You're not scoring any debating points here. Or does it have to get ugly?" In the last sentence, her voice dropped like an anvil to the head.

"I'll deal with the situation," I said.

• • •

Laura Shorewell

"That's cute," I said. "But this isn't a joke."

"I'm not paid to be funny," Scott said. "I understand."

"Be serious."

"Anyone who takes anything about high school seriously is a madman."

"I'm not a man. You don't care how this looks, fine. I do. I can be replaced, and if you act like this, you'll be replaced too, if not for this then for the next thing. I know when to look away." To not know what I know. To not want to know what I know.

That startled him out of banter mode. "What? What do you mean?"

"You know what I mean, about you and girls, and you know what a real investigation will find."

"I haven't done anything wrong."

Everyone has done something wrong when you look closely enough, especially if that someone is a man.

Fucking Scott. Still thinks he's the high school smartass treading the line between getting suspended and taking a stand. Get in line already. This is not the *New York Times* defying the federal government over torture. If—when— parents get ahold of this shit, they're going to roast my ass, which will in turn force me to roast yours.

If I have to talk about conduct unbecoming a teacher, I will. There was that one teacher who starred in a HUMP movie and another in unsubtle mumblecore. Those were close enough to art to wrap the mantle of the avant-garde around ill-advised nudity. Besides, I was the only one who saw the first one, and in the second one, she was gone before I could tell her to pull her damn pants up.

Scott Sole is not a literary critic or intellectual. The guy runs his very own *Saturday Evening Post* and thinks he's changing the world. Whatever it takes, but keep the porn to yourself.

Scott Sole

On the day I was called to the principal's office I was more concerned with my plans immediately after school than Laura. Kate was all over me, the sun was shining. My novel was still idling in neutral, but I was on the verge of getting back to it, like I always was.

And I basically had tenure, which meant I couldn't be fired unless I directed racial slurs at students, slept with students, overslept so often that I habitually failed to show without warning, or otherwise did something of such astonishing folly that I could be a blurb in the *Seattle Times*. Notice how sleeping plays a major role in fireable offenses. A determined enough principal could do me in or force a transfer, but even that could be fought.

If incompetence was a fireable offense we'd lose a quarter of the teachers minimum. Only student demographics make up for pedagogical lethargy.

Still, it was better to hide the evidence than not. I changed the post's date to a couple years earlier and changed its URL too. Google would find it but not anyone looking lazily at the most recent posts.

• • •

Melissa Leon

Laura asked me to her office. Commanded, really. School is more militaristic than is commonly supposed. When I saw Scott leaving it, he looked like a teenage boy who'd been caught taking upskirt shots of his classmates. He walked by me like I wasn't there. I was waiting not to ambush him but to get Laura to sign another tedious form for my degree. Bureaucratic thickets are everywhere in school.

"What's the matter?" I said.

"Oh! Melissa," he said. "It's just this stupid thing—it's nothing. Something that—I guess—I'll tell you about it later." He gave me a funny look, like I smelled bad. He must've seen my unhappiness, which was compounded when he muttered something about "Kate."

"Need someone to talk to?" I said.

"I'm fine," he said, walking again. He bumped into a freshman whose name I didn't know and apologized.

"But—"

He was still walking away and called back, "I'll talk to you later."

At Laura's office I saw Francine, the secretary, had a miniature army of styrofoam cups on her desk. I vowed to never become that person. I vow not to become the thing I hate. Some vows I might even keep.

Laura's door closed, and she turned and almost ran into me like Scott and the student. She wore a maroon skirt and jacket with fake pearls not big enough to be gaudy, a Latina turned empty white bureaucrat. Could still be heading to a hotel for a nooner, though. Seemed like the type: not quite too old, ready for a bit more of life before, you know.

"How's it going with Scott?" she said, slowing.

"Fine," I said. "He's a fine teacher of teachers. Very fine, I mean."

"I was just looking for you."

Her office was the same size as Dundas Gekowski's, as if she was too egalitarian for difference, and it was trimmed in blue—the office, not Dundas—following the rest of Herbert's scheme, with an L-shaped desk that very nearly divided it in half. The desk discouraged invading Laura's space. It signaled remoteness. Two monitors were against the wall. There were pictures of her kindergarten-aged daughter scattered around the office, with some artwork to match, but no photos of whichever guy did the deed. Assuming she was still married to him, or with him, or aware of his existence.

Laura steadied herself, settling her skirt and smoothing her jacket. I felt like a student again, only she was more nervous than me. Or simply good at making everyone around her nervous. Being fired from my teaching internship would be infinitely worse than being suspended.

"I have to ask you a question of a personal nature," she said. "I wish I didn't, but I feel it's important, given the nature of the mentor-mentee relationship. Have you been seeing Scott? Seeing him, uh, sexually?"

How did she know? You can't hide these things, especially from other women. But I didn't want to get in trouble, and after a long beat I said, "Why are you asking?"

"It might be easier to show you."

She turned to her computer and swiveled one of the screens so I could see it passably well.

• • •

Scott Sole

When I walked into my journalism class, I was thinking about how to explain two subjects: why people distrust reporters—for very good reasons—and, in the second half of the class, how to think explicitly in metaphor: we learn one thing in terms of another thing and, by comparing, we see how things are alike and different.

But that was wiped out when I saw Stacy, Sheldon, and a couple others clustered around a phone. Sheldon's phone. Didn't they ever learn? I had deja vu, and when I grabbed the phone from Sheldon I thought back to the unhappy consequences the last time I'd grabbed a phone from students.

Sheldon

Mr. Sole was rattled. He's usually a pretty happy-seeming, arrogant guy who acts like he doesn't care about rules. Teachers aren't supposed to let us eat in class, or drink anything except water, but he said that it was ridiculous to expect us to spend practically seven hours a day without eating.

That day I was texting Ronald Chen, not really thinking except how I didn't fit into these awful fucking seats with the metal bars on one side like a cage. Stacy came over and was like, "Did you see what happened on Mr. Sole's website?" to Ronald.

"What now?" I said. Ronald was hitting me back with some talk about the good shit going down, and I lost track of things. I should've known when the class went ominously quiet something was up. The phone left my hand like it was being pulled by reverse gravity.

When I looked up and went, "Hey!", Mr. Sole was looking down like he'd caught a fish.

Scott Sole

I said to Sheldon, "You can get this back at the end of the day." He made noises about civil rights. They barely exist anymore.

During my planning period, I made the questionable decision to see what else Sheldon had been sent. A picture of a girl. Not Stacy, for which I thanked any deities that might listen to this mortal's pleas. Not Arianna, which is too bad because maybe that would take her out of my hair. Not a refreshing of the video fiasco.

I don't think I would've known the girl on Sheldon's phone, except that she'd already made an impressive name for herself among the freshmen, but not for any out-of-the-ordinary behavior. Sienna. She'd show up dressed like someone's demure grandmother, then change into a short-but-not-quite-mini skirt and tank top.

Sheldon nearly gets busted once for cell phone shenanigans, then he goes and leaves another set of photos on his phone. Only this time, I had a premonition. I kept the phone and thought about calling Marcus and Laura. They were as tired as everyone else about this brand of non-scandal, which will probably, in a decade or two, be little more remarkable than dirty dancing.

I'd hate for Sienna to be collateral damage, but a guy's got to protect his interests, and these days a teenage girl might be the most explosive weapon available.

Sheldon

Mr. Sole asked me to stop by after school.

"Do you know what happened to Arianna Stephenson and Stacy Leon last year?" he asked.

"The whole school does," I said. I couldn't believe I'd never gotten in trouble. Some things are just amazing, like girls who can keep a secret. I guess teachers expect the girls will do it on their own. I tried to get Sienna to do it with a banana, but she said no.

"Have you sent this to anyone? *Anyone?*" He held up the phone with that picture of Sienna on it. That one wasn't mine. It'd been passed to me. She seemed so happy in it.

"No sir."

"Fine. Then I'm going to delete this future felony."

"No!" I said.

"Then I'll give it to Vice Principal Gekowski, and he'll deal with it."

"No!"

"Delete, then?"

"Fine," I said.

"Look, Sheldon," he said. "I don't have a problem with— this." He waved his hand at my phone, like it was a wand from *Harry Potter*. "Your pictures aren't bad, but the legal reaction to them would be. It's like marijuana. Yeah, people do it, but no one wants to get caught. See what I'm saying?"

"It's so not fair."

"Take it up with legislatures and courts, which reflect the hypocritical opinions of the public at large, as well as the disjunction between parents' interests and their offspring's interests. I'm the wrong person to argue fairness with, because I can't do anything to change it."

Asshole. He didn't get what it was like and never would.

Melissa Leon

Laura's mistake was an honest one: Kate looked surprisingly similar to me from the back—but she's got a few more pounds, especially around her hips and ass. The seconds between me realizing that Principal Shorewell thought she had naked pictures of me and that she didn't were long. I began laughing and said they weren't me. The reaction was authentic enough to make Laura laugh too, then apologize. She'd suddenly become worried about the tables turning, with me offended at her. People spend time being offended by each other.

"If there's anything I can do to make this up to you, let me know," she said.

"There might be," I said.

"Go on."

"Offer me a job."

"You know I can't do that right now," Laura said. "Seniority."

"Yes, but you can also wait until the summer and make an emergency hire to avoid those issues." Life really happens in deals and money, not love, despite what the poets rage.

"You're a quick study," she said.

"Just the kind of person you need."

• • •

Scott Sole

I imagined how Laura Shorewell firing me would play out. I could make it easier by getting on the local news and announcing that sex is not a crime. That wouldn't be enough to shock. Better to publicly favor student teacher love, or man-boy love, or just love in general. Then I wouldn't have an excuse to avoid graduate school and making a real mark on the intellectual life of the country. Get started on that novel. Get started on the rest of my life. Write the open-source software, never well defined, that I'd always thought about. Mark the world. No matter what they say, you don't do that in high school. There isn't enough margin. The kids who'll succeed, will probably succeed without you. The rest, you're wasting your time.

I know how the kids feel: stalled. Maybe they feel stalled because so many of the teachers do too. Like I'd never make it out of the stall. A part of me wanted to get caught. That was the best explanation I could find for my behavior, long after the fact.

Melissa Leon

I admit that, as I was going to sleep that night, I was looking at my own wall and thinking, *That hook didn't look too hard to install, did it?* Try explaining it to your parents, though. I really, really needed my own place, or a guy, full-time, with his.

• • •

Scott Sole

After dating a woman for a while, I get to feeling like someone is always sitting on my chest and it's getting harder and harder to breathe. It's unfair to me and to her, I know, but feelings aren't fair. A girl once told me that when she dumped me. I think she got it from a fortune cookie. Another time I confessed what I thought about dating to my older sister, who merely sighed and said that the number of mature men she knew was in the single digits. I told her mature was boring.

I'm not a player, but I do all right, and when my antenna goes up I tend to spot a target. If I don't hit one target, I hit the one after, or the one after that.

Which brings me to Kate, who was like the female me. At first she was into me like a model into speed. She didn't seem like she'd been socially and culturally conditioned like practically every other girl I'd met. She didn't seem inclined to dissemble about desires and experiences. The wisdom I considered hard-earned on the sexual battlefield seemed obvious to her. She knew from reading *Savage Love* from an early age, which she admitted to. Maybe that's what let her train herself to be so vibrantly, vibratingly alive.

She'd been in the "model" shot for the finished project and paid close attention when I told her about the meeting with Laura.

"What would you do?" I said.

"You don't think you'll get fired?" she said.

"I'm a teacher, we have a union. In Seattle people love unions."

"Lucky bastard. If work knew about my life, I'd be gone. That's what happens working for a girls' sports organization."

"You'll corrupt the seven year olds if you have an active life, and I mean 'active' in the most satisfying way possible."

"So what're you going to do about the hook post?"

"If it's going to be a hassle at school, I guess I'll take it down for good," I said. "Find somewhere else for it."

"Doesn't it feel like capitulating and letting someone bully you?"

"There's a place and time to fight and a place and time to get out of the way. I want to fight for what people want to read. They want to read about sex, not about *The Scarlet Letter*. And I want to write what people want to read, not what they don't want to read."

"Oh yeah? I think you're excited by the possibility of fame or notoriety. You want to be like me. In certain circles, I already am notorious."

I was sitting in my chair, a Herman Miller Embody bought used in college, with arms that made it a poor choice for erotic acrobatics. Kate tapped on my shoulders until I scooted back, giving her room to form a triangle with her legs and stand over me, her chest close to my face.

"Why are you so busy with your hands on the keyboard?" she said. "They should be on me."

"Wasn't this afternoon enough?" I said.

"It was then."

Kate took my hands and ran them along her hips. I loved being seduced away from the computer, to curves no iMac, however sexy, could match. I slid one hand up her thigh.

After, I began massaging her, using the warming oil sold by Walgreens. It's great stuff—a teaspoon is enough for the entire back. Coconut oil also works well. A ten-minute massage lifts me high above the guys who roll over to sleep. That assumes I get the real job done, of course. Otherwise it looks like I'm compensating for lacking vital skills.

As I rubbed, Kate said, "We should find another girl again."

"I like the way you think. We should."

"Have one in mind?"

"Not really." She fluttered her hand. "They're... around."

"Let's work on that." I had the feeling that if I didn't, Kate would find someone else who would. That's the kind of relationship we had, and those kinds of relationships don't last forever.

Arianna

I totally didn't know how I was going to write and re-write the stupid *Scarlet Letter* paper for Mr. Sole's class. He was always so mean to us. He doesn't care that we have better things to do with our time. If I were still with Trevor Link, I'd get him to. He writes okay. For a basketball player. Mandy Johnson, that slut, stole him from me. Every girl is a thief.

Every time I started writing I got bored after a minute and go on Facebook until bedtime. Soon I had a week left, and it was the biggest paper of the year. Mr. Sole's post about the girl distracted me for weeks. I kept going over to Stacy's to work. Stacy kind of wrote a page or two for me. She was a better writer than me. She could write it for me.

We were hanging out in her dad's office, I think on a Thursday. It had all these books in it for, like, inspiration. Didn't get any. They kinda mocked me. You can dance, for inspiration.

Melissa came in with tea, and Stacy went on and on about her paper and secondary sources and symbolism and shit. Then she got up to use the bathroom.

When Melissa turned to me with her teacher face on, I told her the truth, like always.

"Didn't you have to turn in drafts?" Melissa said.

"I got extensions."

"Why?"

"I was having some—trouble."

"Why?"

"With boys. I can't explain it. I don't want to talk about it."

"Come on. Enough milking this thing."

"I said I can't talk about it. I have to go. Where's Stacy?"

Melissa was bothered by something else, I think. She was like Voldemort but less pretty. She said softly, "If something's happened, you can tell me, Arianna. I promise."

"What d'you mean?" I said.

"Anything. Anything you want to talk about."

"Nothing happened."

Yet.

Scott Sole

I stayed late, thinking a little about how the newspaper madness would start by the weekend but mostly about Kate coming over when she finished with new work to try the Shibari knots I'd been practicing. Effectiveness was and is more important than aesthetics. Kate liked being tied, and I learned to like the skill of it, as well as the pleasures of the camera. Every day brought new, subtle variations on old delights. New relationship energy is overwhelming, like surfing a tsunami. Why do people get married? Everyone I know who marries dies inside.

An irritating knock from my infamous and lackadaisical procrastinator interrupted my anticipation and, fortunately, the incipient party in my pants. Arianna was tentative at the door. I invited her in. Would she otherwise be unable to enter, like a vampire? We'd never really recovered inter-personally from her wanting to be in creative writing. I too understood her better than she understood me—she saw me as another random jerk, I saw her as misunderstanding what I was trying to do. She'd sought extensions for almost every paper she wrote and I took the easy route out by giving them.

She let the door shut, and I was tired and distracted enough not to tell her to leave it open, or to notice what she wore. A chair next to my desk kept me from having the two-foot expanse of wood-like product between me and students. It was almost 3:11, the time when freedom beck-oned and, when I wasn't detained by salsa, Dream Club, or newspaper business, I could hit the short bus ride up Broad-way and dip into a blissful nap. Or, that day, sex. Kate was sneaking out.

"Hey," I said to Arianna. "How're you?"

"Okay," she said. "You?"

"I was—remembering—oh, it's not important. Got a draft of your *Scarlet Letter* paper?"

"Uh, that's what I was coming here to talk about."

"Okay," I said, suppressing the desire to say, *Again?* "Re-member what I've said in class: something, however bad, can be edited. Nothing can't be."

"What's that on your neck?" Arianna said.

"Nothing," I said, rubbing it self-consciously like a mosquito sting. Fucking Kate. Why do they have to disfigure my neck with love bites?

"Oh," she said. Then, nervous, "So, I have, um, a question about the paper?"

"Yeah?" I said. A question of interpretation, I hoped. "What is it?"

Arianna Stephenson

I was sweating so much and it wasn't even warm. I'd never done something like this. Other girls do this. I'm not like other girls. They don't get me. If they got me they'd do this too. I read about it online. I'd picked my skankiest tank top and tightest jeans. I could do it. Mr. Sole was that guy.

"What can I do, I mean, about this paper?" I said. I kept seeing that picture from the blog post about the hook. The girl's nice butt. *He's that kind of guy.* In my head I chanted it, pretending to be a cheerleader. I could do it.

"What d'you mean?" Scott said.

"I mean, is there anything—*anything*—I can do instead of, like, writing it?"

"What *do* you mean?" he said again.

"Like, you know—something else."

"No, I don't know. You have to write your paper."

"Please," I said. "Anything. Anything at all."

I bent over some. I was cold in my tank top even though I was so hot, so so hot, it was killing me. He sort of scooted away. I wasn't a roach.

"Look, I don't know what to tell you, other than that I can't be having this conversation, and I need to go."

"Come on. I promise—I—I won't tell anyone. Anyone. Ever. For any reason. If you just—you know. Understand. I can't write this paper."

Mr. Sole stood up. "You should—go, and, uh, write your paper—"

"You know I can keep a secret. Did I tell anyone who held the camera in that video last year? No. It was between me and him. This is between me and you."

"Arianna. This has nothing to do with me. Please, please, back up, or I'll have to call."

He threatened his phone. Call who? This wasn't working the way it was supposed to. I wanted to go further, to take off my shirt like I'd done so many times in many places, but what then?

"I need this so, so bad—"

"No more extensions." Mr. Sole was against the wall, cowering. He could've been Stacy's dog. "We're practically at the end of the semester. And I'm going to pretend we never had this conversation. I strongly, strongly suggest you do the same."

"Please," I said.

"Arianna," Mr. Sole said. "Do the right thing. Write the damn paper." It was like he'd busted out in Martian.

"But I—"

"This conversation is over."

"But—"

"You have to go."

This wasn't supposed to be how it works. It's supposed to be easy, he's supposed to say okay, I'm supposed to, like, do my thing, and that's it? He was saying something, pointing to the door. His finger was shaking. I was such an idiot. Such a huge, gigantic, idiot. I'd never finish now. He was probably still in love with that bitch Melissa or something.

I'd never felt so humiliated in my life. He's the one who did it to me. Asshole. He doesn't understand. No one does. He doesn't care. He doesn't—

I wasn't listening and couldn't talk and could feel tears at the corners of my eyes like it was the end. Stupid Mr. Sole. No one'd ever said no like that before. I say no. Not—them.

The door was behind me as I turned away, wanting to get home as quickly as I could. Someone said my name or didn't. I didn't care. Fuck them too.

Scott Sole

High school students can be subtle like a piano falling on the head. Much of my life had been spent learning to vibrate at sexual frequencies, which is half the art of seduction. I couldn't have been more frightened if Grendel leapt out of *Beowulf* and tried to club me to death. This is the kind of shit teachers *do* get fired for. An accusation is as good as a conviction in the eyes of the public. Union or no I was at risk. Those extensions were a mistake. Looking back on the prior months I saw a series of mistakes.

Those mistakes could form a pattern. Visions of school board denunciations appeared, mixed in with moments of me teaching *The Crucible* to high school students who don't get why it's still relevant and will be for a long time.

"Arianna," I finally said. "Do the right thing. Write the damn paper." She looked like I'd busted out in Martian.

"But I—"

"This conversation is over." I stood up. I can play the heavy. It's not a role I choose often, and for me it's not a fun role.

"But—"

"You have to go."

I wasn't thinking clearly. I was only thinking, I need to get out of this situation any way I can. I imagined myself without a job, on the evening news, being led to a court in shackles, a lawyer making a point at trial. A potpourri of bad outcomes.

When she left, leaving behind only whatever absurd perfume she'd chosen for the seduction, she was on the verge of crying, but I had no way of comforting her. I needed comfort myself, and was on the verge of finding a stiff drink.

I could tell Laura or Dundas, but Laura had already expressed deft alpha-male dominance about the post that I thought I'd gotten away with. But I could see things as she would see them: the post, the mutual flirtation Melissa and I had, the way that infatuation might have been consummated before she began student teaching. Laura's pragmatic enough to know that shit happens when mutual attraction gets started, but she was also pragmatic enough to chuck me if the need arose.

Telling the "right" person was a huge risk: she could tell them that I'd propositioned her, getting us into an ugly he-said-she-said. I wish I'd left the door open. The problem is, nothing so brazen has happened to me in my five years as a teacher. You see bizarre things. None this bizarre.

I wanted to say to Arianna something like, "The fact that you can't complete an essay—which has lots of process and structure underlying it—anything resembling on time indicates you'd probably be ten times worse in a creative writing class, where you don't have anything like the degree of hand-holding you get here." Except telling that particular truth would be to needlessly enflame her.

I'd seen Arianna's malady in its many manifestations. Some students will do anything—*anything*—to avoid writing an essay. I can give talks all day about how to write it: turn off the Internet access and phone, force yourself to sit, and something will come out. If nothing else, retype the novel, noticing how each word falls and wondering why it falls where it does instead of somewhere else. I'd offered to literally let Arianna start typing in my classroom. But she said she'd be okay at home.

They play me like I'm a first-person shooter, but life is not a video game.

Arianna Stephenson

He's a big pervert. Everyone knows that he'll touch you at those dance classes if he can. Have you *seen* him with Ms. Messina? Watch this video. They're at the Century Ballroom. It's kind of blurry but it's so obvious what they're about. Look at it. You can see her butt hanging out and everything. Disgusting. Two teachers practically doing it in front of their students. Gross.

Plus there are those girls who really want to be in his creative writing class. We all know how they really get in. Plus we saw him at *Rocky Horror*, dressed in leather. Plus that—that thing on his blog. With the hook. It's a little bit exciting, but mostly gross. Plus some other stuff I bet I don't know about. A guy who'll do that stuff will do anything.

So I figured he might let me off. I could go to the Institute in Barcelona and meet some cute Spanish boy with an accent. My parents would let me have my car back. I tried so hard on the paper, but it wasn't really enough, plus Sheldon kept texting me, so I got kind of distracted, then *Jersey Shore* came on, and I couldn't stop, not just for a paper. So here I am.

When I rushed out I passed Melissa, who was waiting herself, that slut. She probably liked seeing me cry.

• • •

Melissa Leon

Bill Wilson, who my sister wanted to ride without yet knowing it herself, jumped when he realized I was behind him as he spied on Scott Sole's classroom through the glass cut in the door. Nosy prick. Transparency talk is everywhere and it's overrated bullshit.

"What're you doing?" I said.

"Nothing!" he claimed.

"What's wrong?"

"Nothing, Meliss, er, Ms. Leon."

I practiced my teachers' skeptical scowl.

"Are you waiting for Mr. Sole?"

"Kinda. I'll, uh, try again." He scurried off like a cockroach in the light. Parts of New York still have cockroaches—I saw one in the sixth-floor walkup of a DJ I hooked up with. The next morning I learned the DJ was little more attractive than the cockroach. Some of us make more sexual mistakes than others.

I peeked myself. Everyone has a little of the spy in them and every classroom door at Herbert has a glass cutout, five inches by twenty-four inches. It gave teachers the sense that someone might always be surveilling. In that sense classrooms were like being on the Internet.

Were a desk properly placed, however, an observer wouldn't have the angle to see the teacher. Laura had given a little talk about how that's an undesirable setup, but there's not much they can do if the teacher wants to have a desk against the blind corner. There are legitimate reasons for such a configuration.

Scott didn't arrange a blind configuration, not totally. By assuming his vantage point I could see that Bill Wilson had been spying on Arianna. She was hunched over like she'd been defeated, and Scott was pulling away from her like she stank. Arianna got up and turned to the door. What the hell was she wearing? Even by the standards of her peers that was a getup. I didn't see what happened next because I pulled back, since I didn't want to get caught spying, as I'd caught Bill Wilson. I tried the door. Locked. Weird. Why?

Women can sense something about two people that can't be verbally described but is easily recognized. Sexual tension wasn't quite right for what I felt between Scott and Arianna as there was something if not sexual then at least taunt in their body language towards one another.

That, and the locked door.

Arianna. Arianna? *Arianna*. I didn't want to believe. No. She was such an idiot. I didn't know why my sister was friends with her. Or, I mean, I *did* know, because they were both outcasts for doing the kind of shit that gets college girls dates.

I felt this tightening in my chest. I hadn't seen anything. I hoped.

Scott Sole

I thought about skipping out on salsa club, since Arianna had rattled me worse than I wanted to admit to Lola, who taught salsa with me. But I needed to act as normal as possible, given what I was pretty sure had transpired. Ignoring the situation might make it go away. Doing nothing is an underrated course of action. Going to Laura would generate that paper trail. If Laura called in Arianna, Arianna might lie like she had about getting into creative writing. What then? What would Melissa say? Stacy? Marcus? A district attorney?

I didn't know, but I did know that giving Arianna a fat F for English if she failed to turn in her paper could cause problems. A charity C might solve my immediate problem, as long as Arianna turned in something—anything—resembling a paper: two pages long, filled with grammar mistakes, and utterly without an argument.

At the upper gym about 30 students had gathered to discuss the nuances of dancing on two instead of one. Lola was waiting near the entrance.

"A little late today?" she said.

"A little."

"Did you disagree with something you ate? You don't look good."

"Something tried to eat me and I disagree with it."

It was a testament to my habit of cryptic, borderline nonsense pronouncements that Lola didn't ask anything further.

"Can you lead today?" I said.

"Sure," she said.

Salsa dragged, and I didn't have my usual sense of optimism about making a difference at the margins. Trying to get the boys to dance is easier, slightly, than trying to get a dog to fly. They're curiously reluctant, with their cool radars on hyper-alert, and even in an age of supposed tolerance there's still fear of anything that smacks of being gay.

How you can worry about your heterosexuality or lack thereof when dancing with shocking closeness and intimacy with sometimes shockingly nubile girls is strange to me. Status is fickle.

At four the club broke up. Lola put a hand on my shoulder when we were locking up.

"You need to talk to someone, honey?" she said.

As much as I yearned to I shook my head.

"What's the matter?"

"If you find out, it'll have come true, and if you don't, it won't have mattered.

Kate Everett

I work the world's most boring job at a nonprofit dedicated to improving girls' sports. It's a job, I got it by accident, and it leaves me with lots of time at night. Working for a charity makes people think I'm saving the world when I'm mostly pushing paper. In Seattle, as many girls play soccer as boys.

It's not a real important job. I get way too much time to surf the Internet. I went from looking at a little porn now and then, like lots of girls, to checking out the best sites for an hour or two every day, watching the clock until I can sneak off to see Scott after work or Tom during lunch.

Tom: we'd met at Specialty's Bakery when he caught me staring at him and came up to compliment (and perhaps complement) my style. He had this... sparkle. I don't know. It was the best five minute conversation I'd ever had.

Tom had the advantage of being nearby and having his own office in the Smith Tower—he was working for some startup, too nerdy but liked it when I showed up to get it. He snuck off when his cofounders weren't paying attention.

At nights his time disappeared. Maybe he had a serious thing going on, but I hadn't seen a ring. He said I'm the coolest, most understanding girl he'd ever met. Was that true? Was it a compliment?

I told my girlfriend Abby about what was happening—not the *dirty* dirty, just enough to get the idea, and she shook her head. I'm the party girl who knows where the meaning of life is, she's the one with the boring boyfriend she might marry. She'd just say, "This is going to end badly."

It's obvious advice and somewhat true. Sooner or later they're going to find out about each other, or I'm going to break it off with one. Or they're going to meet and it's going to end awesomely.

When Scott texted me that day in June I couldn't reply because my boss was having me look over some copy about a tournament. Then he called. It was serious or Scott was bored. He left a message. When I got a chance I checked: "Hey Kate, there are some things going on here, and I want to touch base. Call me."

He sounded droopy. Based on Scott's flat tone in the message he left, I thought for sure he'd found out about Tom, somehow, and I almost didn't meet for happy hour at Zig Zag downtown. We'd be okay and there was just some misunderstanding.

Arianna Stephenson

I tried asking Stacy's sister for help too, but she's gotten so mean and bossy. She'd become a teacher. One of them. No one would help me. I had to help myself. I had to make Mr. Sole help me. I knew what he wants. I did. I do. I'm not that kind of person. But I can give him what he wants, if he'll give me what I want. It was hopeless.

I kind of didn't know what to do after Mr. Sole's classroom, so I figured I'd warn my mom I might not pass English. Would I still be able to go to Barcelona for fashion camp? The camp wasn't until mid-July. The conversation didn't go so well. When I told her about how I needed to talk to her, she thought I was, like, pregnant.

By the time I got all of it out—how I'd gotten the extension and kept blowing deadlines and was looking at like a couple days left to write a major, researched, 15-page paper—she was telling me how I should be more responsible and why'd I waited and on and on etc. I was ruining my life and if I didn't understand that now I sure as hell would way sooner than I expected.

The next thing she did was pick up the phone and call Herbert, hoping to catch Mr. Sole, but he wasn't around. She said it was practically criminal, and that we were going to go have a talk with him about why he hadn't told her that I'd had all these extensions. It was in a way his fault.

Kate Everett

I was waiting for Scott at Zig Zag, the bar part, talking to an older guy who was way into our conversation—pretty young girl in the land of Amazon drones—and disappointed when Scott showed up to kiss me, long, on the mouth, and cup my ass. It made me want to leave right away. A heat flowed down there and as often happened I felt terribly, horribly, physically empty.

"What up, babe?" he said, all cool pretending.

"You're the one who said you needed a drink," I said.

"You aren't gonna believe what happened."

"How d'you know?"

"Because if someone told me, I wouldn't. I continually underestimate the perfidy of teenage girls."

"Perfidy?"

"It's a great word in the right situation that basically means liar. In this instance, a student."

"Liars, all of them," I said. "I know, I was one. Claimed I didn't masturbate when I did it every day and three times on the weekends. What's it this time?"

"Kate," he said, making me nervous by seriousness unlike him, "Do you want to make this thing official?"

Great. Every guy thinks when he offers commitment he's got a fucking pot of gold. Every one of my girlfriends waits for this moment, and I always get it. Can't men take their neediness somewhere else, and bring it back to me in a couple years when I'm interested?

"Why're you asking me now?" I said.

"So that's a no."

"It's a question."

"It's a no. A yes means yes, anything else means no."

"I didn't say that. You're not yourself. What's wrong? Talk to me first."

He told me a sob story about Arianna offering him sex. At school. In his classroom. He'd told me the story of this girl's video adventures, and her wanting to get in his creative writing class, and I was like, *She's bad news*. I know bad girls in a good way and the bad girls who are *dangerous*. Scott's so soft at heart, he wants to believe all those students are going to be okay, and I'm like, *be realistic*. Not all of them are nice, some of them are liars, some of them are always going to be dumb. I guess if he believed that, he'd quit being a teacher.

"What would you do if you were me?" Scott said when he was done with his story and second drink.

"Tell the principal," I said. "It's almost always better to tell than not to tell. You'll be protecting yourself."

"I'm not sure I will be. I want to bury my head in the sand and hope everything goes away. In the news teachers get in trouble for minor stuff all over the country." Of course I read the news. Jerk.

"You haven't done anything wrong."

"That's not how it works. It doesn't matter if I do anything wrong, it matters if I *look* like I've done something wrong."

"This isn't going to affect things between us, is it?" Anymore than the inappropriate ejaculation about us being offended.

"No, of course not," he said.

I leaned over to whisper alcoholically in his ear, "We should get out of here and find something else to do for the next hour. You're so uptight. You need to relax." I squeezed his inner thigh to make my point. He flexed to make his.

"You're right," he said. "I've had enough."

"That's great."

The question hung over us. "Is this why you asked me to be your girlfriend?"

"No. I wanted to ask before this."

I didn't believe him.

"Can we talk about this when you're feeling better?" I said.

• • •

Scott Sole

Kate as an official girlfriend, to be paraded as soon as possible, might deflect suspicion, but not if she wasn't down for the struggle. Which she'd said, not in so many words, she wasn't. I thought again about going to Laura. I'd have to be nuts not to. I'd also have to be nuts to. A Kafkaesque situation.

How would the conversation go? Not well. "She said what?" "That she'd do anything—with a sexual overtone." "What does that mean?" "You know—like she'd hook up with me if I let her off the hook." "But she didn't say so?" "Not in so many words, no, but that's what she was getting at. We both knew it." They'd think: *Is it the girl, or is it the teacher?*

I couldn't blame Laura and Dundas. That's what I'd do in their position too. Nothing personal. It's just, with material like this, you want to stay far, far away. The kind of thing the *Seattle Times* would kill you with.

That night Kate came over, and we did our thing while I thought about whether the phone was going to ring, and when Kate was dressing to leave, I asked if she wanted to stay over. She said sure. Then I asked, "Is there someone else?"

She went from focused on getting her bra settled to thoughtful. "Why do you ask?"

"That's the only reason I can think of for why you wouldn't."

"Scott, I like you. I like you a lot. Do I ask what you do when I'm not around?"

"No."

"Then I don't want you to ask me what I do when you're not around."

"That's an inherently unstable arrangement. Besides, to be honest I haven't done anyone besides you since a week or two after we got together."

"Very romantic. Do you keep a log in Google Calendar?"

"Kate. Don't be like this."

"You want to make it official because you're worried about this girl."

"No." Yes. Was I this transparent? Was everyone? I could sense the other guy, or guys in the plural given her appetites, lurking in Kate's background and she could no doubt sense the anxiety in mine.

"Scott," Kate said. "Being desperate is never attractive."

I didn't do anything with Arianna and was never tempted. Pussy is never worth jail. Instead, I focused on Kate, who was in front of me, gorgeous, willing, happy. We did it again with her on the hook, made dinner, made love. Kate had to leave because she said something about waking up early.

When I woke up, I hated the situation I'd wandered into and thought about whether I'd have a job when I got to school. Spies and drug runners must feel the same way, never knowing if they're walking into their own death.

Herbert was eerily normal. But there was a message on my school voicemail: Arianna's mother wanting to have a meeting as soon as possible. So that would be the hammer's vector: through me, not through Laura. It seemed unlikely that Arianna had lied and told her mother I'd made a pass: if she had, the mother would go straight to the cops. I called.

The mother picked up and explained that Arianna told her about the *Scarlet Letter* paper and the extensions and how she wanted to find a way out of this mess, and she wished she'd been informed before. She suggested a meeting right after school, and I agreed, feeling almost as triumphant as I had the first time I saw a pretty girl naked.

I felt free all day, energized by the prospect of negotiating and getting to summer without a major crisis. Arianna and her mother, Gail, showed up as promised, with Arianna being dragged along like she was a dog being dropped off at the pound.

Gail was one of those women who turns spawning into her entire life's work. Arianna seemed like the sort of person who'd rail against her parents to seem cool up until the moment she needed something or had an unpaid phone bill, the kind who'd complain about how they didn't understand her even as they paid outrageous credit card bills.

We had some preliminaries, and I gave Gail a copy of the assignment—the same one I'd distributed back in January, at the beginning of the semester. I admitted that I should've called her earlier, but Arianna kept saying she'd get it done, just next week.

"You have to understand," Gail said. "I don't see how she could've had this long to write a paper and not done it."

"She kept making promises, and I kept letting it go because she said she was having some—personal problems," I said.

"That's not good enough. You should have alerted us to this earlier."

"Look, Arianna is what—17? I agree that, in retrospect, I would have preferred to inform you."

"Why didn't you send a letter, or an email, or call me directly?"

"Look, I can't send a letter for every student who misses a deadline."

"I don't care about every student. I care about Arianna."

The conversation continued in this vein for a while, until we got to the point where Gail was saying, "Let me be more blunt: is there anything we can we do to improve Arianna's grade on *this* paper and in this class?"

I'd been in similar situations. I knew what she wants, and I knew what I should do to make this problem go away. It would be easy to fall on my sword. America's schools are so bad in part because teachers practice defensively so as to avoid problems like this one. Something perverse made me want to teach a lesson about honesty and work. About how important I am, how they can't fuck with me. A stupid and petty power battle, but one you've probably fought with teachers, bosses, coworkers, even when it's against your own interests.

Politicians, CEOs, and celebrities will evade responsibility as much as or more than their children, so it probably shouldn't be a surprise when the people who admire them—which is to say, almost everyone—mimic what they see on TV. If I wasn't convinced Arianna was a champion evader before, her stunt certainly made her one.

I knew I could've ended it by saying, *We can come to an arrangement*, but I didn't say that, because I'm an idiot and I wanted Arianna to know that she couldn't get away with shit like this.

"No," I said.

Stacy Leon

Arianna stopped responding to texts for like two days. It was so bad I called. Nothing. Sheldon texted that she wasn't replying to him or to Facebook posts. He'd left on her wall, "damn girl where you bbeen? I keep wanting to see u. L8r."

I left some too, like, "girlllllyyyyyy I hate this paper. When we do it?"

Nothing.

I was worried enough that when I saw Bill Wilson after school, he asked what was going on and I told him about Arianna.

"You guys are pretty close, aren't you?" he said.

"Kind of," I said. "It's … complicated."

"Yeah. I saw."

"Thanks, jerk." I knew he had a crush on me and was too scared to ask me out.

"Look, I hope she's okay," he said. "I liked her in Ms. Messina's class."

"I'm going to find out what happened soon."

"You want company?"

I paused. It was almost tempting. Bill hadn't gotten flustered when I called him a jerk. He acted like it was part of the conversation. When had he learned to look me in the eye like that? I wanted to say yes—it would be good to talk to someone real—but I shook my head.

"You change your mind," he said, "text me."

I went over to Arianna's to try to get her out of her shell. It took twenty knocks and doorbell ringing before she appeared. Her face was blotchy from crying. No parents home. I went inside, wondering what was up.

"I can't do it," she said.

"What?" I said. "I can't understand you."

"Write the paper. This stupid, stupid paper. I would give anything—*anything*—not to have to write it."

"Why?"

"My mom knows and he won't give me another extension."

"Who?"

"Mr. Sole. For the *Scarlet Letter* paper."

"Arianna," I said. "What happened?"

• • •

Arianna Stephenson

Stacy again. I wished she'd leave me alone. I wish everyone would. I have no friends.

"What's wrong?" she said.

"My parents took away my phone and cancelled our Internet access. They said I wasn't doing anything until I wrote a whole entire paper. In, like, two days! How am I supposed to do that?"

"One letter at a time."

"Shut up! Shut *up*. Shut UP, SHUT up, shut up," I said. "I know. You don't have to be such a bitch."

There was something wrong with my face and Stacy came over to hold me.

Stacy Leon

I tried to get her to write her paper for like two hours. Her parents came home early—they weren't happy to see me but they were happy that we'd gotten almost a page done, with me pretty much telling her what to write.

Partway through, Arianna gave up and cried. I didn't know what to do. She curled into a ball like a little girl. I was disgusted. Arianna had gotten herself into another mess of her own making. It's like she's not even smart enough to have any idea what she's doing. I'm not perfect, but compared to her I'm Einstein.

She was also babbling.

"He didn't do it," Arianna said. "I thought he would."

"Who didn't do what?"

"Mr. Sole. He's just. He's just."

"What?" I said.

"I—I mean he did. He tried to."

"You're not making any sense. Take time. Enunciate. Breathe."

I patted her back. This was the same girl who'd been so eager to get naked for Sheldon? The fuck?

"He told me that if I did, I wouldn't have to, you know, write the paper. That's why I got that time."

"No, I don't. Who are you talking about?"

"Mr. Sole."

"What did you do?"

"You have to swear," Arianna said. "Swear on everything, that you won't tell anyone."

"I swear. Tell me what you did."

"No—he did."

"Go on, already."

"He told me that if I—did things with him—he'd let me not write the paper."

"Did things? What things?"

"You know," she said. "Things like on the video."

"Did you?"

• • •

Arianna Stephenson

I wanted Stacy to leave me alone, and I thought if I told her those things she would. It didn't turn out that way. She said she was going to tell my parents.

I grabbed her and tried to wrestle her to the floor. I'm bigger than she is. It didn't work, because she wedged me against the door and was gone before I could do anything. The bass of her feet on the stairs was like that scene in *Lord of the Rings* where they're underground and there're drums.

My door was still open, and I got up to shut it. It was all my fault. I don't know why Mr. Sole didn't make me write the paper. He assigned us this super-long paper because he's a jerk. He wants me to hurt. I'll never have to write when I get out of stupid school. English is stupid.

I heard low, urgent voices. Stupid Stacy. What was she telling my parents?

This time, two sets of feet went *doom doom* up the stairs, and I got the feeling I was in big trouble.

Stacy Leon

Arianna's parents swore me to secrecy. They didn't like me, because they thought I'd led Arianna into the video mess, and whenever they saw us hanging out I could tell they wanted to say to Arianna, *She's the bad girl*. It's amazing how people still think about the bad girl like that. Especially me. I mean, you should've seen Brooke Hargreaves. Guys *still* go on about her.

What Arianna did reminded me, like so many things do, of Mr. Sole. In creative writing, he's always going on and on about how people have characters, and if you can't recognize character in real life, you're going to have a hard time repro-ducing it in fiction. And this didn't seem right for him. It was out of character. He was careful to stay away from stuff like that.

Yeah, Scott told some dirty jokes in class, and told us we could call him by his first name because the false honorific "mister" is a vestigial relic of early twentieth-century propri-ety that remains only in the teaching and legal professions. But it seems like the kind of teacher who'd tell dirty jokes and be so real *wouldn't* try to get a girl to do those things be-cause he'd be worried about how all that stuff in class would come across.

The world is a confusing place and I wished it was sim-pler. As a kid I thought the world works like *Harry Potter*, with the good guys and the bad guys pretty cleanly mapped out. Only a couple people waver in the middle. When I got older, I realized pretty much everyone is in the middle, some are smarter, some are dumber, some nicer, some meaner, but mostly I can't tell, much as I'd like to.

I needed someone to talk to. Sheldon was out. I could imagine him hatching an idea like this, not talking about it. If he knew everyone knew. When I walked into my house I heard Melissa, standing over a stove and making a pot of lentils. Health freak. Maybe she'd seen a scale lately.

"Where's mom?" I said.

"Running late. Why?"

"Can I talk to you about something?"

• • •

Melissa Leon

Stacy never comes to me for advice. She thinks anything she's doing is the first time it's been done in the history of the world. I figured her problem was about boys, hopefully without evidence this time. Unless Stacy had suddenly developed a shocking interest in art or science, men and money were the only things she cared about.

"What's wrong?" I said.

"Can you keep a secret?"

"Yeah, sure, of course," I said. No one keeps secrets in high school, but everyone says they will. "What's wrong?"

"Arianna," she said. "But not in the way you think."

Stacy Leon

Melissa froze when I told her what Arianna had told me and what I hadn't exactly told her parents. We were together for a weird minute.

"Who else have you told?" she finally said.

"You. Arianna's parents."

She stood up. I grabbed her arm. "Don't tell mom and dad," I said. "Please. No matter what."

"I wasn't going to." She went down again. "You think it's true?"

"Don't know. Arianna has a habit of making things up."

"Just because someone's cried wolf, doesn't mean there's not a wolf at the door. I don't know who to believe. When did this allegedly happen?"

"Arianna didn't say. Pretty recently."

"These kinds of accusations, Stacy, do you understand how—in our society—the—never mind."

My mouth was dry, and as much as I kept drinking water, I couldn't get it to un-dry. Melissa, who usually looked over my shoulder when she's talking, was staring at me in the eye, but like I wasn't there. It freaked me out. I wish this hadn't happened to me. I wish Arianna could've talked to someone else.

• • •

Melissa Leon

People can grow, but they can't fundamentally change. Not quickly. Another Scott-ism. He didn't seem the type to offer sex-for-grades arrangements: he cared too much about knowledge and was too scrupulous about not getting into this kind of trouble with students. Except me, but that was different, I was flirting with him, and by the time it happened I'd practically given him my sodden panties and told him how bad I wanted him. It was disgraceful, but abject I'd been. For the right guy. What is that they do to make me like that? He could get it elsewhere and wasn't desperate enough to scheme for it.

He had this wild streak. I don't really know what to call it—atë, I guess, as the ancient Greeks did. It's this sense of madness and delusion, usually uncontrollable, that can strike even very normal people. It banishes reason and makes people become one with the raging passion that lurks inside of each of us.

I experienced it that night with him and Kate: atë fueled by alcohol and by me needing to really feel something. The overly intellectualized part of our society has a big problem with feeling, with touching one another, with letting go of the mind. Neal Stephenson calls cerebral people "geeks." Ecstatic experience is forgotten. A long time ago Scott forwarded me this little editorial Stephenson wrote, "Turn On, Tune In, Veg Out."

But atë lacks the premeditation Scott would've needed to make the offer he did. I don't know how long atë can last. I do know that I liked and didn't like the things I saw in Scott when he let go. Like I liked and didn't like the things I saw in me.

Scott Sole

It's hard to say how high school students will turn out. Most are very poorly formed. And poorly informed. My high school teachers no doubt thought me entirely average. Time has proven them mostly correct. Every year that passes makes me a little less certain that I'm going to finish that novel. It's one of these adult disappointments, the kind they don't warn you about in school, where everyone can do everything if you want to badly enough. What they don't tell you about is the people who want it badly and still don't get it.

Arianna, I have to concede in the name of fairness, might turn out okay. More likely than not she'll become one of those vapid, pretty girls who can get away with it now but don't realize they're not going to forever. Adults could never warn her of this, of course, because she wouldn't be smart enough to listen.

I was ruminating, which is a bad habit but better than smoking, when my phone rang. Melissa.

"Hello, gorgeous," I said. "Just who I was thinking about."

"Cut the crap," she said. "Leave Arianna out of your … advice, whatever it is. She's got enough problems as is."

PART V

Dundas Gekowski

Melissa Leon came in, looked around the office at the crap carpeting and child's drawings on the wall, along with a movie poster reprint of Samuel L. Jackson being righteous in *Pulp Fiction*. Reminds the kids of how I imagine myself and how they should see me.

I remembered her as a student. Didn't know how to dress herself then, but every so often she'd come to school in a sundress in the spring, or a tight co-ed sweater and those leggings. We're supposed to ignore that stuff on a student, but what do you want? Guys can't check manhood at the door. No wonder we can't get male teachers for shit. Between the manhood check and the kumbayah BS, I wonder what I'm doing in the administration. The classroom is where the magic happens. In admin I'm just ratface, the repository for people's problems.

I was tempted to get botox or surgery to fix the thing with my face. But I'm already married. Baby number two is on the way.

Melissa and I exchanged pleasantries. She asked about Columbia, my first daughter, who'd been sleeping through the night. Smart girl. Melissa, I mean. Butter me up first. Parents love talking about their kids. Never understood why till I had one. So much is hidden until it's experienced. Everyone else's experience doesn't prepare us.

"So what's the problem?" I said.

"My sister's friend," she said. "Arianna Stephenson. You know her?"

"Sure, sure. Problems with clothes and cameras."

"I know the feeling," Melissa said. "She's also got a problem with—authority. With Scott. Let me log on to Facebook from your computer so I can show you."

"Hang on," I said. There was no way for me to log out without her figuring I was logged on. Like being naked. Filtering software blocked Facebook and similar sites, but staff have an override password.

"Do I want to see this?" I said.

"Think so," Melissa said. "It's not bad, it's just mean."

She came round to my side of the desk. A metal beast. I don't know how it started life, but it had a file cabinet for one set of legs and a keyboard tray I welded to the bottom myself. Let Laura's room be the nice one. Melissa bent over, unselfconsciously, to type her user name and password. Once she got in, I looked under her shoulder, and I got a picture of Melissa, in a group of girls, all holding up red beer cups like Viking steins, grabbing their boobs with their other hands. Could've been taken yesterday or five years ago. I decided not to ask. Don't want to know everything.

She found Arianna's profile and showed me where the girl said ""i hate mr sole hes such a dick" and some other, nastier things, mostly about how he was going to give her a bad grade and didn't like her.

"Reads like standard teen venting to me," I said.

"She still shouldn't be talking about him like that," Melissa said, and for the first time I wondered seriously if the rumors were true.

"You know we can't truly police what they do off school grounds."

"No, but you can scare them."

"You show this to Mr. Sole?"

"Not yet. He's got enough problems."

"You're worried that if Arianna is right, and he doesn't like her, this'll make him like her less."

"Sort of."

The moment beat. Melissa squirmed like the student she used to be. Silence has its utilities. Melissa broke first.

"Will you do it for me?" she said. "As a favor?"

"I'll talk to Arianna," I said.

Someone knocked on the door. It was Arianna's mother, with an unpleasant man in a suit.

Scott Sole

An unknown 206 number flashed like a threat. Enough weirdos and students have my number that I almost didn't answer. Could be an irate boyfriend. But I'd hung up on Melissa to take it, and that made it irrationally necessary to answer in my mind.

"Hello?"

"Scott? This is Dundas. Normally I would ask how you are but right now that does not matter. I wish I had better news, but I'm calling to ask you not to come to school tomorrow."

I said, "There's what—a week of class left? I just collected final papers. The *Hatchet* is going to bed in two days. I'm on the home stretch. The computer science final is my last real project."

"Policy is policy," Dundas said. "I'd rather you hear it from me: there's been an allegation of misconduct on your part."

"What?" My heart began pounding like I was in a Victorian novel. Visions of lawyers swam across my eyes, with me crusading for the rights of—of who? Kate mouthed: Who is it? I ignored her.

"Conduct of a—sexual nature."

"What? That post bullshit?" The standards teachers are held to are absurd. It's like we're not people—we're supposed to be Disney characters.

"No, I mean with a student. It's very serious. A female student at Herbert has made an allegation against you. I can't say more. You'll get the formal notice tomorrow. You may wish to contact an attorney and your union representative."

"I've never slept with a student, and I never will," I said. Besides, thinking of Arianna's offer, if I were to, I'd only do it with a student smart enough not to need to trade sex for grades.

"I believe you," Dundas said. His voice was so flat that I couldn't tell if he did—he'd assumed the drone of a robot. "But I also have to tell you that the police have been notified of our investigation and the allegation."

"Fuck, Dundas," I said. "You serious? On what basis?"

"The student's allegation. It's standard procedure, as you know. It's policy."

Besides Arianna there were less obvious candidates, like Alanna Guildhall, a somewhat unbalanced journalistic writing student who I trusted less than Sheldon. Or Melissa. I couldn't fathom why she would, unless she was jealous of Kate or some other girl. Given that most Western literature is based on sexual jealousy, I guess I could understand.

"Tell me who," I said.

"Privately," he said, "I wish I could. I'm sorry."

"Does Laura believe me?"

"Laura's following protocol. Belief is irrelevant as you know. We have no choice but to take all allegations seriously."

"A student can, at any time, completely fuck with your life by opening their mouth, and when it comes out they're lying, nothing bad happens to them."

I could practically hear the shrug from Dundas. He didn't make the system. What were you going to do? The world is what it is, and if you want autonomy over your affairs, start a business. Being part of big, politicky institutions means playing by their rules and their desire to denude sexuality.

"You there?" I said.

"I'm here," Dundas said. "Don't know what you want me to say."

"I know what I want you to say, but you're not going to say it, so it doesn't matter, does it?"

"Good talking to you, Scott, but I don't see us talking much in the immediate future. Good luck with all this. No matter what happens, you're a hell of a teacher."

"But, Dundas, who—"

The line was dead, like my professional life. "Conduct unbecoming a teacher." What the hell does that mean? Are teachers not allowed to have sex? If so, you can fire most, but not all, of us. With every drug store selling vibrators and lube, what's wrong with a little bondage? Without a concrete act, I'd hope to get out of it.

"What's the matter, honey?" Kate said.

• • •

Melissa Leon

I'm not sure what I was expecting when I picked up the phone. Scott taught us to introduce ourselves and state our purpose, but Lauren Reitman left a vague message saying that she was with the *Seattle Times*. It got me excited. Maybe I'd have a summer job better than working at Starbucks. I could go beyond asking if you prefer half-caf or full-caf—like it matters.

I'd applied for a temporary job as an "Internet Data Analyst," which was a fuzzy term basically denoting someone with enough technical skills to do simple programming tasks, like setting up databases but with enough writing skill to function as a reporter. I had some poorly formed ideas about soliciting community experts who know something special or unusual about Seattle and having readers vote on the results. Exciting stuff for new media types, but maybe not so much to the rest of the world.

I called her back as soon as I got out of school, and without preamble she hit me:

"I'm calling to get your side of the story and to see how your romantic relationship with Scott Sole got started. I gather that you two became romantically linked after book club meetings at Herbert High, while you were still a student."

"No!" I said. "I wasn't a student." And then I realized my mistake, but it was too late to rewind the tape. They say your mind races in situations like this but mine died. "I mean, I've never been, you know, with him. With anyone like that."

"Do you know if Scott Sole has a pattern of being extremely friendly with his female students?"

"Of course not. He's friendly with everyone."

"Is it true that he helped arrange for you to receive your current position as a student teacher at Herbert?"

"What? I don't know what you mean."

"Can you elaborate on how you got your position?"

"I applied, I got it."

"I understand that's a very desirable placement, given Herbert's demographics relative to other Seattle schools, like Rainer Beach. Especially in an economy like this."

"I have to go," I said. "Goodbye."

"Wait!" Lauren said. "Is there anything else you'd like to add?"

"I never had an affair, or a relationship, or whatever, with Scott Sole."

"Even though he admitted you did?"

"He what? No. I mean. Never mind."

"Then—"

I'd been tricked, like a dumbass 16-year-old. I hung up. It happens so slowly on the page and so fast in real life. The same number flashed me. Scott couldn't've told them. That'd be too much even for him. Yeah, life was transient and possessions pointless and all the rest of it, but the guy didn't have a death wish.

People also sometimes say things like, "My whole world was turned upside down," and I always used to think they were just lazy writers who couldn't find an original comment. Now that my whole world had turned upside down, I empathized. And started thinking about where I might get a job.

• • •

Lauren Reitman

I'm a reporter for the *Seattle Times*. If I get laid off, as so many of my colleagues have been over the last ten years, I'll join an online news startup, or begin blogging full-time and starve. Whatever it takes to be a reporter, I'll do: food kitchens, giving up my MacBook, walking in the rain without a Gore-Tex coat.

A source—whose name I can't reveal—gave me a tip about what was going on at Herbert High. The source was vague on what had exactly transpired but pointed to a specific person of interest, and the source was credible enough to make me examine the situation. It's a dangerous thing to investigate: rooting around sexual issues can create them where they don't exist, but the reality of what people like to do when they think no one is looking remains. After I spoke to the source, in person and over the phone, I was sufficiently convinced to gather some preliminary facts using methods I would rather not discuss.

My editor, David Wong, liked the short presentation I gave about what I'd learned and the overall trajectory of the story, and he said I could spend a couple hours looking for more solid information. Working at a newspaper means you're always counting pageviews—Google is the most powerful force in news—and readers like nothing more than stories about sex among people who aren't supposed to have it regular: teachers, preachers, politicians, parents. We get outraged when they're getting what we aren't.

Once I started, mapping the key players at Herbert wasn't very hard, even with the limited connections I had at first. Frankly, if some of the more lascivious rumors repeated to me were true, the girl involved had to be protected, using whatever means necessary. Teachers have a serious responsibility to their students, and that responsibility must not be violated.

• • •

Scott Sole

Kate became preoccupied. Texts went unreturned or languidly returned. I sensed a shift that was sudden, though I didn't see its suddenness at first. Like so many things it was evident only in retrospect. She didn't want to see me for an afterschool quickie one day, which I interpreted as a sign that she'd found someone else to fill that space. Wouldn't be hard for a woman of her talents, who leaves many men hard and some hard up. For a guy, it is almost always better to assume yes until an explicit no, but her disappearing said what her words didn't.

I wasn't ready to mention it when she did come over—in time for dinner but not as early as she once did. The timing made me wonder. It's great when I'm the feast, not so good when she's eating at another table.

She arrived half an hour to an hour before Ryan came home from work, and we made it on the kitchen counter. No undressing beyond the necessities, the action asking: What is going on between us? Our bodies synced like iPhones, but our emotions—that kind of data doesn't transfer so easily.

We finished up, ate some tasty dal, retired to my room, maybe to watch a movie. I'd bought some Bose Companion 20 speakers and was eager to try them out. Not that a movie like *High Fidelity* would do much to test them, but they had to beat the iMac's speakers.

Before I could get the movie queued, Kate said, "A reporter called me today."

"Which one of my students?" I said. "I'll threaten them with retroactive Fs."

"Not a student. A real one. From the newspaper. She was asking about you."

"She cute?"

"This could be serious."

"What'd she want?"

"She was asking how long I'd known you, about your online dating history."

"I hope you told them it was as long as my—" I looked down at my lap to indicate.

"Not real impressive, then."

"So they find my Love Lab profile," I said. "Free country, etc."

"Haven't you," Kate said, "deleted your Love Lab profile?"

"You checked it lately?" I said.

"Yeah ..."

"Then you know: how long has it been since I logged in?"

"A while."

"Right. Since like a week after we first hooked up. When was the last time you logged in?"

Nothing.

"Let's find out," I said. I rolled back to the iMac. Kate jumped up and grabbed my arms.

"Please," she said. "Let's not."

"Why? Hold on a sec."

I shook her off, wondering if she was going to try to force the issue. You can't hide information for long. Love Lab tells you the time since someone behind another profile logged in. The idea was to keep people looking for fresh matches and avoid sending notes to stale users. The unintended side effect was a *pas de deux* of online courtship: when to stop scanning for other options? It's a delicate online moment, like a Facebook relationship status change.

As I checked for what I could already guess, Kate said, "It's not what you think."

"Funny," I said. "I would believe you, except for what you just said—saying 'It's not what you think,' makes me think it's what I think."

"Huh?"

"Nothing." Nothing was kind of how I felt, too. I should've been angry. But it would be unfair to be angry. Kate didn't feel like she was sitting on my chest, like most girls do. I, like most guys, can bang any girl for six weeks, no problem. After that, even if she's gorgeous, I find it harder and harder to want to be harder and harder. No one does it all the time. Relationships consist of the other bits. If I wanted to be really, cruelly honest, I'd say that Kate was a lot, but she wasn't Melissa. Close in age, close in looks, close in everything but what counted most. She probably thought the same of me, or she wanted more adventure than I could give.

"I wouldn't've logged in at all," Kate explained.

I went, "This, from the girl who's exploring her sexuality with most of Seattle? Which I approve of, by the way, it's only strange, really strange, for you to be telling *me* this. It should be the other way around."

"Good. Then we can have the talk."

I groaned. "I *hate* the talk. Can't we just continue like we've been doing?"

"Sure. If you don't mind me continuing like we're doing in other places."

"If I didn't want to make you happy, I wouldn't do the things I do. Isn't that obvious?"

"I need more."

"I don't know how many extra girls I can find on short notice, Kate. A guy's got other things on his plate."

"Not that. Scott, I need to be your girlfriend."

"Or?"

"Or I have to move on. My mom warned me, guys will lead you on forever, and the ones you want the most will be the most reluctant to commit."

"You crazy? You've been hunting cock on Love Lab like it was your job."

"I was wrong, and I want us to think about a different sort of relationship—"

"Kate, you're self-selecting for perceived alpha males who have other options: if they don't want to commit, they're good enough, and if they do, they're not worth your own commitment. You've caught yourself in an apparent paradox. One that a lot of women seem to like."

"Enough verbal games. What about a different kind of relationship, an open one? Verbal games are your way of avoiding saying anything."

"Too much time in novels, which are just giant constructs of verbal agility that have no meaning whatsoever in the real world." Except that they teach you how to live.

"You're doing it now. That's how much I know you."

"After a couple months of messing around, you *know* me?"

"I know you avoid real emotional engagement. Like the one I'm making you have right now. What's it going to be?"

"Define 'it.' "

"I'm not a student, not one of his, here," Kate said—although in a way we all remain students of life, all the time.

Right then I didn't have students, not students who paid, which is all that matters; I had pointless papers. "This isn't class, where the teacher scores debating points for pointless philosophy. If you want to fuck your students, or your former students, or whoever, that's fine, but don't fuck with me."

"I admire your verbal dexterity, using fuck in two senses. You've been hanging out with me."

"Are you going to man up and make me your girlfriend?"

"On open terms?"

"It's not terms, it's rules to make things work. For both of us. I know myself and I think I'm starting to know you."

I tapped my lips. Like an accountant. An accountant of love. Something had happened between the hot sex in the bathroom and this conversation. Life, I guess. Before I could respond my phone rang.

Melissa Leon

I texted Scott to call me then called him. He didn't pick up, the jerk, and like an hour later he called me back and said, "What's up?", all cool, like I was just some chick from the Internet.

"Scott," I said. "I have to tell you something. A—"

"Pregnant. Shit. What should we do?"

"No, I'm not pregnant. A reporter just called me."

"Oh. What'd he want?"

"*She* was asking about us."

"About us?"

"I mean, about whether … we've ever been together?"

"And you said?"

"No."

I heard a girl, giggling, in the background. Fucking Scott. So glad I wasn't carrying that man's child.

"How'd she know to ask?" he said.

"Exactly."

"What's her name?"

"Lauren Reitman."

"Hang on."

I heard typing. Scott had one of these noisy keyboards with a funny name—Model M or N—that clack like an old-fashioned typewriter. Part of a cool pose. He needed a beret. If he actually wrote for an hour or two a day, he'd have a novel to show me instead of a novel to talk about. Him and writing was like a fourteen-year-old girl and sex.

"She's written about the Seattle Public Schools before," he said, "but it looks like most of her stuff is obits and human interest. So-and-so died, cat stuck in a tree. Crap. But how'd she know?"

"I don't know. I didn't, obviously. Who else could know? Stacy, Arianna, maybe Sheldon if they've talked to him. I've never admitted anything to them. Can we get together and talk about this in person?" It was disconcerting to imagine him batting Kate away while she was sitting next to him in lingerie. Or worse.

"We'll do it tomorrow morning," Scott said. "If she only now called you, she's on a fishing expedition. We don't have anything to worry about. Chances are this whole thing'll blow over. It's silly. There's no story."

"Is there?" I said.

"No."

"I'd rather talk about it tonight."

"Me too, but I'm tired, my feet hurt, and I want to veg out and read a book. Lev Grossman's *The Magicians* is promising, and I have it sitting next to me."

"What else do you have sitting next to you?" I said. "A big ole skank?"

Instead of getting ruffled, he laughed. Laughter defended him from everything every woman had thrown at him. "That's uncharitable. There's someone on the other line. I've gotta run. Later." I could hear his theories in my head, about how females denigrate their rivals' sexual fidelity as a means of mate guarding.

"But, Scott, what about—"

I stopped mid-sentence. The line was dead. Asshole. He'd get what he deserved.

Bill Wilson

Arianna's never going to like me like she should. She gets with all these jerks. But I felt it was my duty to report what I'd seen. It's important to tell the truth. She'd never understand that I did it for her, but I was hoping to tell her about it. Maybe during the summer, when we'd have time to hang out. I had to save her. I'd have to talk to her some more, but, you know, this was better than doing nothing.

Arianna Stephenson

This chick called and said she was from the *Seattle Times*. I talked to her a little about Herbert. When she asked out of the blue if I'd been sexually harassed by a teacher I froze.

I literally couldn't move. I didn't know what to do, so I did nothing. That asshole Bill Wilson? The creeper chick went, "Hello? Hello? This fucking thing. Fucking AT&T," and hung up. I didn't pick up the second time. I was like, Who gave her my number?

Then, like practically as soon as that happened, there was this knock, and I desperately wished I wasn't alone.

"Who's there?" I said.

"Seattle Police Department," a woman's voice said.

I peered into the eyehole. They were wearing blue uniforms and made me scared. One guy and one woman.

"What do you want?"

"We're looking for the Stephenson residence. Open the door."

I didn't want to but I did, just a little, and the woman stepped up like she was going to force it the rest of the way.

"Arianna Stephenson?" she said.

"Yes?"

"Do you have a parent or guardian with you?"

"Not, like, right now," I said.

They looked at each other like that meant something, and she said they were investigating a crime. I wanted them to go away and to un-say everything that I'd said so that things could go back to normal and I wouldn't be in trouble. Fucking trouble. I always find it. Being an adult means not having to listen to assholes.

"We need to ask you a few questions about a criminal investigation. Open the door."

I didn't really want to talk to them. They kept asking, like, a million questions. I felt like I was on TV. I can't even remember what they said. They'd had like an hour to talk to me until my dad came home, and we all went quiet in the living room.

He looked like he'd walked into a drug-fueled orgy. Fuck. The cops introduced themselves. I don't remember their funny names. I wanted to die. My dad got mad at them and at me. He told them to step outside with him. They didn't want to, and after a minute I heard dad raise his voice. He doesn't do that. He's soft.

He said they couldn't talk to me without him or my mom in the room. A couple minutes later, my mom showed up, and when she saw my dad talking to cops, she got kind of angry. I wish I'd told them more about what was going on first. Everything was so confusing. More things happened but I don't remember them. It's so easy to block.

Dad came in and said, "Next time, we're getting a lawyer."

Scott Sole

I called Marcus. He was a cop. They might've gone through him. Our friendship, based mostly on jokes, picking up women in bars, discussing the game, and *The Game*, must be worth something. He didn't answer. I called every hour until he picked up, a few minutes after ten.

"You gonna hit me all night?" he said. "A man's got to get his rest."

"Marcus," I said. "Have you heard?"

"The Mariners, they doin decent this year. With Lopez on the mound—"

"Don't kid. You know what I mean."

He sighed. "Scottie, you know I'm not supposed to be speaking with you 'less you're in an interrogation room, right?"

"I understand," I said. "It's your job, and you can't come between a man and his money. I get it. I just want to know—"

"You got it, you wouldn't be phoning me at this hour."

I heard feminine laughter in the background. "Company?" I said.

"Yeah. She's already satiated, though, so we can speak as men for a moment. But she hungry again, quick, you know what I mean."

"Yes, yes—I'm asking as a friend," I said. "Who? Who did it?"

"No friends in a time like this, my man. If I could help, I would."

"If our positions were reversed, I'd help you."

"Would you?" he said. I could picture him on the other side, running his hand across his shaven smooth bald head, like he did when he was thinking or nervous. He must be wearing one of those shiny shirts he liked, like he was a billboard. "Coming up, I heard that around. Most often, I heard it when a young buck was going to jail and his buddy was putting him there. You hear me?"

"No. What's this got to do with anything?"

"I was in your shoes, man, you'd not pick up the telephone."

"That's not true!"

"I hope not. Look, friend, get a night's rest, call your folks, get a lawyer. You have a right to speak to an attorney, right? You hear it on TV every day. That's all I can tell you."

"A lawyer?" I said. "I don't have enough money for rent most months."

"What can I tell you, my man? Lawyer's cheaper than time in jail."

• • •

Arianna Stephenson

"I thought only people who were guilty of things got lawyers," I said.

"No," my dad said. "People who're innocent get lawyers too, because it's possible—very possible—to be falsely accused, arrested, and tried. If you read the news, you'd know. Second of all, lawyers are there to protect your interests. Third of all, you want someone who deals with cops and judges every day. In some fields, a mistake is something you don't do next time. In others, a mistake can land you in prison."

"What're my 'interests?'"

"Not having your name dragged through the mud because of that damn teacher."

Given what had already happened, I thought it was a little late. People had started posting shit on the Internet, saying I'd wanted it from Mr. Sole all along. Even Stacy didn't believe me. She said she thought I was lying like I always was.

"Oh," I said.

"Also, after your Internet stunts, there's no guarantee prosecutors won't become interested in you."

Weirdly, the only person who kind of believed me was Melissa, and I had no idea why.

My dad found a lawyer named Meyer Shapiro. The cops were kind of surprised when he came with me. They were like, I'm the victim, but my dad was like, always get a lawyer when cops are around.

This time things were much shorter, and the lawyer guy kept interrupting things they said, talking about my privacy and fragile state of mind. I was like, You have no idea.

Kate Logan

You know how you want it sometimes, bad? That's how it's like all the time for me. Guys *say* they like that. Until they're confronted with the real thing, they probably believe they'll like it. Then they see it and not everyone can handle it. When I was the age of Scott's students guys were all so exciting. When I saw them up close I realized most guys aren't really good or bad. They're merely disappointing.

By the time I got to Scott, I'd exhausted the dateable among friends and friends of friends and had grown tired of losers in bars. I don't get the girls who want to hook up with smooth morons. I guess that's why they get good and drunk. Me, I'd rather skip the drinking and go straight to the action.

Except I like a guy I know, rather than a procession of one-offs. I want a relationship. I want security and excitement. Scott I thought could be into the same.

The Internet offered a solution to the bar and friends-of-friends problem. It offered an infinite number of horny nerds. Just my type. Scott was one, and he was all talking big about his books and how he likes a girl who likes what she likes, but it got to the point where I was realizing his own life was so messed up that he didn't really know what to do with mine. He wasn't going to stay with me, "official" bull-shit or open relationship or whatever, so I should try again. Story of my life.

• • •

Scott Sole

I woke up late, wondering about what the hell to do with my time. My life was fragmenting, and if I had to tell the story of that hellish week, it would be fragmented too.

The unemployed have it rough. No structure to their lives, or to what became "my life." "Paid administrative leave" was the technical term, but I'd already assumed the unemployed state of mind. On Marcus's advice I searched the Internet for "Seattle defense attorney," "Seattle defense lawyer," "Seattle defense lawyer sex," and similar strings.

The possibilities felt endless. I was in a haze and struggling with the paradox of choice. I called some firms and left messages on their night lines. How is a guy supposed to pick a lawyer? On TV they just materialize next to the defendant, the lawyer in a suit and the poor schmuck in an orange jumpsuit. Humiliating, really. I'd never make a decent showing in orange.

The prices were terrible. Lawyers start at $250 an hour and go north. Should've gone to law school. I could spend as much in a day as I make in a month of teaching. I had $20,000 available through credit cards. Maybe I could apply for a couple more. I got enough offers in the mail. Do lawyers even take credit cards? I hoped so. I applied for two more, thinking I was making progress. Better to take the cards and declare bankruptcy than to go to jail. Finding lawyers is a tedious, annoying process facilitated fortunately by Google.

I picked one named Tommy Killian who sounded like a bulldog and had a blog of his own, where he discussed the ins and outs of criminal cases he'd worked on in a way that I found comforting. Good blogs signal confidence and transparency. He told me some obvious stuff, like not to talk to cops, and that if they hadn't gotten in contact with me they almost certainly would soon.

I called Melissa. She'd be at school, unless she was suspended too.

"Scott," she answered, clearly unhappy, "How are you?"

"Before you hang up, I want you to know. It's not true. I don't even know what 'it' is yet."

"Scott, what's happening to you?"

But I had already hung up.

Three days into leave the intercom buzzed. Melissa's voice floated through our phone, asking to be let in. Kate would never do something like this. I let her in and prepared myself as best I could for the inevitable emotional storm. It was barely after school, yet it felt like midnight.

She looked frazzled, and a bit wet from the rain. Her usually straight hair stuck out at odd angles. She rushed into my arms and asked what was wrong, like she'd been watching film noir.

"I don't know," I said. "Dundas called me, said a student made an accusation of a sexual nature against me." Hearing his bureaucratic language through another person's voice made me ill anew.

"Who?" she said.

"Don't know."

"What was the accusation?"

"I don't know that either—"

"D'you know what it could be?" Melissa said.

I hesitated. Arianna had probably found a way out of her grade predicament. It seemed preposterous that she'd lie and say we'd had sex, and that people would believe her. But whenever a guy is falsely accused of rape it must feel preposterous. I knew a guy in college who was accused by a girl who, years later, said she thought he was overly aggressive and went to the police saying he tried to rape her in order to teach him a lesson. I don't think Melissa would look kindly on Arianna as an answer, however, so I lied and said, "Not really. Dundas won't say." Her skepticism was as palpable as a crashing wave to the face.

I went on, "A lawyer told me not to talk to anyone, for any reason."

Never did I make a worse mistake than not getting Melissa on my side. Maybe if I'd said yes, Arianna would've stuck to the agreement. Sometimes the right thing is the wrong thing.

Melissa quizzed me on the Dundas conversation, as if she'd become a detective overnight. Like an idiot, I emphasized what he'd said about the police, even though I knew I shouldn't talk to someone who could implicate me. Melissa wouldn't, though. I didn't believe she would, with the situation spinning fantastically like a drunk girl in an alcoholic haze.

After an hour, Melissa made to leave. But I didn't want her to. I did something stupid and immediately regretted it: we made love. She was so filled with authentic feelings that I couldn't resist kissing her when I saw her eyes widen with fear and concern.

She'd been waiting for it too, like she knew Kate was a transient phenomenon, like she knew where my heart lay all along. We were swept up in the passion of the thing and barely got to my bedroom, where Ryan wouldn't see.

"What happened?" she said, half during, half after.

"I told you, I don't know." There is no real reason why people do the things they do or are attracted to the people they're attracted to. At best we make up stories after the fact.

"I mean, between us?"

"I don't know that either."

"Me neither. I wish I did." Analysis. Sometimes it fails. There are limits to verbal life.

"You can stay over," I said in a rush. "You're a student teacher. I guess—I don't know what I guess. Or guessed. You have a tentative job offer for next year, if you can get the emergency slot."

She shrugged. "I shouldn't stay," she said, reaching for her sexy but not too sexy, almost everyday really, underwear. Some women demand decently sexy underwear all the time. She must've rushed. Or this was spontaneous.

The only thing I can think about what I said and did next is that I wasn't thinking clearly. To be fair, I doubt anyone would under the situation. I was exhausted by the wondering, and I said, "No, please. I need someone with me tonight. Won't you?"

"I have to get up tomorrow. For school."

"Your bag," I said, gesturing. She kept long pants and a shirt in there for emergencies. Modern girls, you have to love them, ready to go straight to work from a hookup's house.

"I shouldn't," she said.

"I know," I said. "But won't you do it anyway? For me?"

I'd never displayed this kind of vulnerability to her. She had this momentary look of triumph, like she'd finally won the race I didn't even know she was running.

• • •

Lauren Reitman

The easiest source of information about a student is often other students. I asked around some, checked Facebook, and learned the victim's primary friends.

A couple of judicious phone calls later and I found enough evidence, combined with the school district spokeswoman's official statement that a teacher had been put on leave, to go to my editor. I presented the case in 1,000 words. He said it was bullshit and to give him 400. Not hard. Not hard at all.

Laura Shorewell

These hero teachers think they've walked onto a movie set and are going to change lives. They never last because the reality is too brutal. They also usually turn out to be major pains in the ass. They're too close to students and when they realize what the students are like, they quit or they change to the point they're not hero teachers anymore. Teaching is about endurance. Doing it de-romanticizes it. Teachers in it for the long haul are trying to get a decent cup of coffee, get through the day, get home to their families, not screw anything up.

I'd thought Scott had moved past the hero phase and into the more typical phase of seeing students like bottles on a conveyor belt. But no, he had to go get involved in his students' lives, which parents hate and the media can use. In these matters I had no choice. The choices had been made long before the mess got to me.

Speaking of newspapers, I told the bitch-queen reporter, "No comment," and I warned the chain of command.

Everyone knows what the fucking media is like. No one wants to be headline news because the headline news is always bad. The more money stolen or the more salacious, the better to watch other people do what you secretly want to do. I'd heard Scott give his talk about the cathartic aspects of community punishment in *The Scarlet Letter* and had no doubt that he was thinking about that very point when he wasn't thinking about lawyers.

I didn't see any reason to go down for a grown man who should know better and know how to control the snake in his pants. If it's true. If it matters if it's true. Once it's in the *Seattle Times* and on TV, it's true if it's true or not. True as a live grenade. The only thing you can do is take cover, which is exactly what I did and you'd do too if you were in the circumstance.

There are good reasons teachers stay very far from their students. I shouldn't have to enumerate them. On some level it means leaving students to fend for themselves, but if they don't learn in high school, where will they? I've heard Scott rant about how weird it is that we lock students in school for eight hours a day and expect them to somehow imbibe adulthood and maturity from each other, but you know what? It doesn't matter.

We live in the world we live in, not some other world where students, I don't know, learn adult behaviors from adults they're working with instead of cruel, childish behaviors from one another, when they're trapped in a world of fake work that most of them intuit correctly won't matter a whit for their ultimate lives. But you can't tell that to the heroes, to the ones who think they're messiahs. You can only wait until they realize they aren't. Scott took the hard road, and I'm sorry for him, but it was his choice to act the way he acted. Act guilty, people think you're guilty, that's how it goes.

• • •

Scott Sole

Everything in life is a choice, of course, although sometimes we choose to deny that we have a choice. We make them every day, by the hundreds or thousands, and we live, or don't, and we turn them into literature or music or art or a poorly timed outcry into the tangled darkness of the Internet.

A pair of official district investigators, a white guy and an Asian woman, arranged to meet with me and a union rep, at my inconvenience. Killian agreed to come too. Billable hours. I was going to have to beg my family for money and sell my ass to gay men on Capitol Hill.

Killian himself had an office not quite in downtown—too expensive—but in Ballard, still close enough to reach the courthouses. His office wasn't plush yet seemed a place where Things Got Done. He was a medium-height guy, built like an army grunt, with an oily smile and ready sneer. A guy who would've been found in a boxing ring once upon a time and now found his outlet in a courtroom, which to him was much the same thing. I'd never make it as a lawyer. I like looking at all sides of a problem too much, and the law rewards picking a side and ravaging the other into submission.

The meeting itself was boring, foreordained, bureaucratic. The interesting part was how much they'd found in a short period of time: text messages, most of them kind but overly intimate in a non-sexual way, emails about newspaper stories, the post about how to put up a hook. Suspicious but not damning. Enough ambiguity to make a primed reader wonder. Enough to make me think it was going to be a long time before I got my job back, if I ever did, and the only hope I had was in the power of the union to protect me from unfair punishments meted by moralistic administrators.

They were moralistic opportunists, reflecting parents and the spotlight. I had heard tales about Laura's days of drugs, sex, and pleasure. More than once, Dundas and I had stopped talking to watch a teenage girl's fine ass or plump prominent jiggling breasts as she walked by. Money and jobs on the line can change a person very fast. Dundas told the truth when he said we wouldn't likely be talking again. If we did I wouldn't be talking to Dundas, but Dundas's bureaucratic avatar.

There's no specific rule in the 339-page, small-print teaching guidelines against teachers sending texts to students. The texts and emails didn't offer or solicit sex. Some texts were to and from Stacy, so they'd gotten to her, too.

I'd never been tempted by Arianna or Stacy. Stacy wasn't her sister. To the right person they were pretty but I wasn't the right person. But I could see how texts could be read as the townspeople read the Letter on Hester's breast, and how Hester is cast out because she becomes a sacrificial receptacle for the community's sins and desires—desires they cannot admit to themselves.

The Facebook posts on Melissa's page came back to me, including the suggestion that editing is best done in person. The investigators thought I was implying "editing" meant sex. Had they ever done any significant writing of enduring value? Most people haven't.

When I said goodbye to Killian in the afternoon, I went for a drink with Lola, who had a tabloid vulture's eye for drama.

"It's a damn shame," Lola said when I told her about the texts. "You never touched her, either?"

"No," I said.

"Would you tell me if you had?"

"Would you tell Laura?"

"No."

"Would you think less of me?"

"Scott, what d'you think?" Lola said.

"That's fair," I said. "But I didn't."

"Have you ever?"

"No. Not like that."

"Good."

"Have you?" I said. "With a student?"

"No. Not like that," she said. "What now?"

"Tommy Killian said that until charges are filed, I should sit tight. Charges might not be filed. Prosecutors only like filing in cases they know they can win, and mine isn't a slam dunk. The union guy said this could drag on a year or more. A transfer might be the negotiated solution. I don't know if I have it in me. And if I get back, the kids have all heard the rumors, they allude to the past."

"If I could help you," Lola said, "I would. But there's nothing I can do, especially with the police."

"You being here is enough," I said, raising my glass. The Alibi Room whispered around us, and to me it whispered about memories of Melissa. I wondered if Lola was actually reporting back everything I said.

• • •

Arianna Stephenson

I didn't realize, once you start telling people a story the thing gets this movement.

Momentum, I mean, of its own. I thought, "I can say this and it'll be okay," except it wasn't. Every time I opened my mouth, something else went wrong.

So I decided to close my mouth for good. My parents kept saying that I had to follow through, cooperate with investigators, and they'd go back and forth between whispering at me like I was a stupid dog and screaming like I was their prisoner. Mr. Sole sometimes said that believing in freedom and your own autonomy creates freedom, but it wasn't easy when your parents are, like, We're going to kill you if you don't talk.

I kept saying, I don't want to, I prefer not to, let me go, and it took them a while but they got the message. I don't know what the school people did. I didn't care. They'd taken enough of me from all those interviews. Leeches. Mosquitos. All of them. They'd suck me dry in a second. I dreamed of Barcelona. Guys are different there.

During the summer I found the Running Start application. The same one Mr. Sole had given me after the video. He kept them on his desk like the health teacher keeps condoms. Maybe I really did need a change of scenery. I'd need to take tests. I'd missed some deadlines but who cares? I was pretty sure I could get some rules bent, considering what happened to me.

• • •

Scott Sole

When I got home from drinks with Lola, Ryan was there, back early from his job as a paper shredder. I said hi, despondent, and Ryan looked as bad. He told me that the district's investigators had shown and asked all kinds of questions about me, most of them related to students and sex.

That got my attention.

He not only answered them, but made them coffee in my Chemex using my beans, an Ethiopian dark-roast blend from Stumptown. They asked about Melissa in particular, as well as a girl who'd graduated two years before named Hailey Radway. She'd been the editor of the News section and a favorite because of her unusual wit and her wholesome aversion to Facebook.

We kept in touch electronically and kept completely out of touch physically, beyond the occasional hug. She'd found a boyfriend named Justen the first week of her freshman year at Washington State. The boyfriend was a computer science major and looked suspiciously like me. Ryan seemed like such a bit player in my story and the story of my life, yet he might prove shockingly decisive to its conclusion—maybe because I'd ignored him, and he was somewhat jealous of my sex life, while his greatest commitment was to Internet porn.

He'd put on weight, which wasn't surprising given his fast-food diet and exercise regimen of sometimes getting up for a soda. Living like an average American yields the results of an average American. Which is to say, not much action in bed or on the trail.

I should've told Ryan more about what was going on, so he might've stayed silent instead of being silently jealous of the not enormous but reasonably active number of attractive girls who paraded through, sometimes forgetting to put on more than one of my T-shirts when they left my room to get water or eat.

The scene was much longer, much more drawn out, and much more pointless, because he'd done what he'd done: tell them about Melissa. When a stranger asks about your sex life, the best answer is usually no answer.

I sent Melissa a text asking her to call. I wanted to be more specific, but texts are forever while voice, usually, is here and gone like a slice of sun. She didn't reply, which wasn't surprising given the hour. I waited, then called. It sounded like she was at the closest bus stop to school, on 23rd.

"Melissa," I said. "I have to ask you a question."

"I feel I should ask you some, but you go first."

"There were some people from the district who talked to Ryan, and he said some things—about us. Did they talk to you?"

"They did."

My hand began trembling. It hadn't done that since I'd begun asking out and undressing girls as a teenager. Nerves are failure.

"What'd you tell them?"

"Nothing serious."

"Did you tell them about—us?"

"Us?"

"You know—five years ago. After you graduated?"

"You know I *want* a job after all this is over, right?"

"Right."

"So why the fuck would I tell them? Do you think I'm stupid?"

The hand ceased. "Thank you," I said.

JAKE SELIGER

"They did ask a lot of questions about the movements of you, Stacy, and Arianna. I answered those as truthfully as I could, without telling them anything real."

"You don't believe it, do you?"

"I don't know what to believe anymore, Scott. I believe that I knew you at one point. I believe that I loved you at one point, not very long ago—"

"I believe you still love me," I said. "If you didn't, you wouldn't be on the phone with me, talking. Look. I know the Kate thing was a mistake. I'm sorry about that. If I could take it back, I would."

"Would you?"

"Yes," I lied, through the heat and curves and memory of her body. "For you, I would. Because I know what's in your heart. If you hated me, you'd have told."

"And hurt myself in the process. Right."

"You wouldn't be the first woman who perceives herself to be scorned and goes on a self-destructive rampage in response. Shakespeare has one or two of those." Since women are usually the ones who say yes or no to sex, it makes them very, very angry when men say no, since it removes the validation so many of them crave. It didn't seem wise to share that insight with Melissa.

"I'm angry with you, not stupid. I know you have a thing for stupid girls with big tits, like every fucking guy, but I thought I could live with that. How's your slut, by the way?"

"What?"

"Your slut—Kate?"

"I thought you were too big and liberated a person to use that word. Too sexy."

"When the label fits, it fits."

"No more, 'I'm so opposed to the double standard that I'd never deploy it against a rival?' Does competition make you sink that low?"

"I can only tell you what's true in life."

"I don't even know what that means."

"You don't have to," Melissa said.

"We're talking in circles," I said. "I wish you hadn't said *anything* about Stacy and Arianna, but I suppose that can't be helped now."

"How could I not say anything about Arianna, after that day she left your office crying?"

"She was propositioning *me* for sex that day—she'd fuck me if I gave her an A on her unwritten *Scarlet Letter* paper."

Silence. Of the sort usually modified by the word "stunned" in novels.

"I said no, of course," I said. "Contrary to popular belief, men are not driven solely by sex. I'm not, at least. With you, I was driven by you being attractive, yes, but other things too, all of which Arianna lacks in spades. I did it because I love you."

"Then why'd you encourage me to go to NYU?"

"Sometimes, if you love truly someone, you have to let them go. Pop songs get that right. You were 18. If I'd tried to keep you for myself, keep you from your dreams, how long would I have succeeded? A year? Two? At what cost? Do you know how many girls go to college with boyfriends who don't last out their freshman, let alone sophomore, year? What would people have said, us getting together that fast? No: I did it because I had to, not because I wanted to. Just like I'm falling back on the clichéd language of love songs to express my feelings. You needed that other experience. Few if any of us are meant for only one or two partners." Conversations with Kate on this point flashed back to me. Who knew what man Melissa was speaking to at the same time she spoke to me.

"That might be the most romantic thing anyone's ever said to me."

"Love isn't turned off like a spigot, and even when the plant withers, a seed that could be watered remains."

"Are you asking me out?" Melissa said.

"You have a fantastic way of shattering the moment," I said. "I thought we'd made a breakthrough, and then ... 'Are you asking me out?' "

"Are you?"

"Under the circumstances, it would be best if we stayed away from each for the time being. Ryan—he told them so much. It's all hearsay, of course, as long as you don't corroborate it. I might get out of this yet."

"Yeah?"

"Yeah. I get out of things like you get out of lingerie."

"Truly, your romantic talk has returned."

"Silence is golden, Melissa. Have they rescinded your job offer for next year?"

"No, but Dundas told me that I'm on thin ice with the district. The axe might come down anytime."

"If it does, will he at least write you a decent rec letter?"

"I already asked—how'd you know?"

"You might still be okay, in the end, even if I'm not."

"You'll be okay. You're a guy who lands on his feet."

"I'd rather land on my back, with a nice mattress underneath me and good company on top."

"Dirty boy," Melissa said. "It's amazing you lasted as long as you did in the classroom."

"I teach the lessons that count: how to live and why. Lessons that go undelivered, marked 'Return to sender.' By the way, your use of the past tense there is highly inappropriate in this situation."

"Every moment I've spent with you is highly inappropriate."

"Isn't that what you like about it?"

"Yes. Isn't that what you like about meeting strangers from the Internet for sex?"

"Everyone is a stranger the first time we encounter them," I said. "The question is, what does it take to make them into a friend?"

"You're so ridiculous," Melissa said. "You just want to get in their pants."

"I want human connection—isn't that what this is all about? Isn't that what computers and cell phones are supposed to enable? Getting into someone's pants is only one kind of connection. Could be the most fun kind, but there are many others too."

"Yes. I'm looking for them."

"Besides, if I'm driving you so crazy, why haven't you done the obvious and found another guy, since the last one I mean? The city's crawling with them. Throw a stick and hit a dick. It would require you to smile on the bus occasionally, ask a guy what he's reading, but it can be done, you know, *you* want it."

"It doesn't work that way for me," Melissa said.

"Sure it does. It works that way for everyone—only question is, do you acknowledge it, or do you live in a fantasy world where the rules of social life only apply to everyone else? Love is. I want to chase girls *with* you. I think you have the proclivity."

"Your obsession with the underlying structure of mating markets is doing bad things to you. But if you weren't so good to talk to, I wouldn't've missed two buses standing in the drizzle with you."

"Is that why you told—because of my interest in why people do who they do?"

"No."

"Is it because you love me?"

I could hear her smile on the other end.

Melissa Leon

I saw the *Seattle Times* article the next morning, a week and change after Scott disappeared and a full-time sub showed up, and it was terrible: a female student at Herbert had accused a male teacher of sexual improprieties. Not only that, but it said, "A former female student is now under the male teacher's supervision as a student teacher, but she denies any inappropriate relationship." In news-speak, that translates to giant fluorescent arrows pointing at my head. Never trust reporters. I'd denied it to that awful reporter, when it came down to it.

Reitman said Scott had a history of making "off-color comments" in the classroom. Whatever the fuck that meant. It had some quotes from his blog that must've been ten years old. When Shannon and him wrote about how to sleep with your T.A. if you've got a crush, he was 18—the same age as his current students. (His advice was good, too: flirt with them, wait until the semester ends, then move in for the kill. Don't be subtle. Smart T.A.s won't put their career on the line for some ass, but if you hand it to them on a silver platter, many will indulge. I'd kept that in mind at NYU.)

I don't need help with or protection from my sex or sexuality. Neither does Scott. He was attracted to me for my mind and my body. If he wasn't, we wouldn't still be together. I'm sure he's had offers like mine. He's a kind of cute guy, and if you're not into meatheads or emo losers, you don't have good choices as a high school girl.

None of the guys have any sophistication whatsoever. High school girls can date college guys, mostly during the summer, and then have them dump you as soon as they get back to campus. Campus is a giant girl pile. Too many girls are there, sodden pussies aching, competing for too few real guys. Guys have lost the ability to be guys.

The idea that teenage girls are too stupid to decide who they want to have sex with is bullshit. I know people say I'll have a different point of view when I have kids of my own, but they're full of shit too. I hope my own daughters are smart enough to make their own decisions about who they sleep with and who they don't.

Scott Sole

My social network turned against me.

Teachers with any personality tell the occasional joke or story they wouldn't want to see in the *New York Times* or flashed across the bottom of CNN. If they have any passion, they show emotions they—we—probably shouldn't. Teaching becomes personal because life is personal. People aren't giant antiseptic asexual corporations in miniture. When they try to mold themselves in the image of giant corporations, they lose more than just what makes them special.

I mean, I had a physics teacher in high school who told a story, for reasons hazy to me now, about his college roommate's girlfriend, who he dubbed the "screamer." Not the sort of thing he'd want on YouTube, but we loved him for it.

No one would want to defend every moment in the public glare. Mentioning that it's ridiculous not to let teenagers in Babeland, asking (jocularly) a guy if he's only learning to play the guitar because he thinks it'll get him laid, telling a brief Halloween anecdote about a friend who turns into a stripper when drunk—these aren't everyday occurrences. Ask around enough and you'll hear about them.

Lauren Reitman, I gathered, had asked around enough to hear about them, and when I was accused, every one of those moments came under undeserved scrutiny. Not the ones where I stayed late to edit an essay or the unpaid hours I spent rewriting ineffectual lesson plans handed down from district offices and state bureaucrats.

Teachable moments often aren't defensible. They're a little part of the random flow of experience. Mine just became lodged in the eddy of media scrutiny, pretty much guaranteeing that the slog back into the river of normalcy would be a long one.

Lauren Reitman

The guy dug his own grave, as they say, by leaving his writing hanging all over the Internet like a fat man's gut over his belt. My only question was, how'd no one figure this out before? He wrote a sex column for *The Daily*, him and some busty chick. Shannon. Now she's on Facebook posting a million pictures of her adorable infant. Her route from college sex kitten to mom was typical and easy. His from campus lothario to shaper of young minds was less so.

On his blog, there were photos of bikini-clad women. For a teacher, really? Have some sense. I checked the exif data, and most were taken with early Canon DSLRs, indicating that he'd been at it for a while. Some had been uploaded to Flickr for anyone to see. Given the wealth of evidence, I'm surprised no one predicted this kind of behavior. The man left a trail a mile wide. If I can find it, why can't anyone else? The story tone was easy: administrations were guilty of a dereliction of their duty to protect students.

Kate Everett

Scott and I were great for the time we lasted.

Decline might start with sex or not but always shows itself in sex. Scott, he wasn't as excited about tying me up. I get bored of most guys before they get tired of me, because they start to seem the *same* all the time—they all experience life as a series of interludes between getting laid.

Scott liked getting laid, of course, but he went beyond that. I don't think I would've appreciated him when I was younger. I hope for intimacy and understanding from lovers but sometimes all I get is a decent lay. That's what I was to Scott, since he was still in love with that other girl. I could never be official given that situation and he couldn't give her up. Lots of girls are too stupid to see they can't compete. But I still liked him in bed, and I liked the pleasure he gave me. I knew he wouldn't make me his real girlfriend. I didn't want him to, really. I wanted to know I was right. I was. I was some story for him to tell at bullshit parties because he's all words and not enough in the sex.

I wish I liked girls better. They're good for a night but not so much after that. They're so full of drama, I want someone who says, "Here's what I want," instead of ten hours of, "Here's how I feel." I don't think he did things with that high school girl. She was just another random dumbass like most of us are at that age. Too bad we don't see it at the time.

The tipping point came when Scott texted me to say he wanted to cancel, that he'd had a lousy day, and I told him bullshit, I'd be over.

When a man cancels afternoon delight, a girl has to wonder if someone else is providing the delight. Did he know about Tom?

He was home. I threw my arms around him and said, "Scott!" He was more hesitant to put his arms around me. I wasn't fucking radioactive.

"I don't know what to do," he said.

I whispered back, "Do you know who to do?" I kept my boobs, not like they were much, dammit, against his chest. He could feel them through his polo shirt. Amazing, what the man will wear in the cold. "What happened?"

"I've been put on paid administrative leave," he said.

"Now you have more free time, right?"

"No. I mean, during the summer I do, but when school starts again I have to go fold envelopes or do database work or something boring like that."

"So what?"

"So nothing. That's my whole life right now."

"Nothing?"

"Nothing."

"Let me see if I can make you feel better."

"Okay," he said.

"Scott, it's not like I'm trying to imprison you here. Are you not interested in me at all? Not interested in having sex?"

"Of course I am," he said like he wasn't.

"How about this," I said. "When you're ready to man up—and I do mean up—and see me, you text me."

"I thought—" he said to me, who was already gone.

I didn't think I'd ever see him again.

Melissa Leon

Getting back together with Scott is what I should've done the day I got back to Seattle but the other guy was there and Scott seemed distracted. The intervening boys and girls were fluff. Nothing wrong with fluff or the occasional sex party. But priorities are priorities.

Scott Sole

An early knock startled me. I wasn't used to unemployment, and the knock hit two minutes before I expected my alarm. I didn't want to get up. I didn't want to believe some asshole was pounding on my door this early. By the time I got combobulated, Melissa was already dressing, like this was an everyday occurrence. By the time I got to my door, Ryan was asking who it was. He usually woke after I'd left for school.

Whoever was on the other side said they were looking for Scott Sole.

"Who are you?" Ryan said.

"Seattle police."

Ryan was startled. I wasn't. I motioned for Ryan to leave and opened the door to destiny.

"Yes?" I said.

"Scott Sole?" they said. Neither had a uniform beyond cheap suits. One, the thin one, had a badge that said "Snow," which made me want to ask if he'd melt under the sun.

"Excuse me," Melissa said from behind me. She'd already dressed in yesterday's clothes. I'd never seen her so expeditious.

Melissa slipped out, keeping her head down and practically covering her face with her coat, like she was the perp. She had to mutter, "Excuse me," to the cops.

The fat one stopped her. "How old are you, miss?" she said.

"Twenty-three."

"Got some ID?"

Melissa rummaged her purse for her driver's license.

"You don't need to show them," I said. "I've read the rulings."

"Spare it, jailhouse lawyer," one cop said.

Melissa found it and handed it to the cop, the fat one. She should've told them to fuck off. People who work in authoritarian institutions instinctively obey perceived authority.

"Leon?" he said, raising his eyes, like he'd seen a chick with a dick when he expected something different.

"Can I have that back?"

"Relation to Stacy Leon?"

"How do you know her name?" Melissa said.

"What's your relationship?"

"Sister."

"I see," he said. "You work at Herbert High?"

"That's where I'm going now, if you gentlemen will excuse me." Melissa didn't ask how they knew where she worked.

She squeezed through them, even though the two guys tried to block her way. They in turn squeezed her breasts and ass with their bodies, arms rigidly at their sides, as she passed. It pissed me off, how they could molest her, but there was nothing I could do, which pissed me off even more. Dealing with cops makes me start to have a glimmer of understanding of how black people must feel.

"We'd like to ask you a few more questions," the fat cop said. "Would you please accompany us to the precinct?"

"I'd rather not," I said. "I have a lot to do this morning—"

I began closing the door. The thin one stopped it with his foot.

"Look," he said. "You can do this easily, and come with us, or the hard way, and wait for us to make you come. Which do you prefer?"

"To consult with my attorney," I said. "One moment."

I called Tommy Killian, panicked. He asked if police were at my door and I said yes. He told me he'd meet me as soon as he could, that I should go with the police, and not say a word until he was right next to me.

Lola Messina

A few days after the first and worst newspaper story ran I saw Scott. That story made him seem like he was running a brothel instead of a classroom. Not that there's anything wrong with brothels. They're hated as much as they're used. I've fantasized about working in one.

I should clarify, too, that it was *The Seattle Times*. A real newspaper, not the *Hatchet*. The *Seattle Times* follows you around Google forever. The article mentioned a possible improper relationship with a student teacher. It didn't take a PhD in bullshit to figure what that meant. Who it meant. I talked to Melissa right away and told her I was behind her 100%. In a non-pervy way.

Frankly, I don't know why or how Scott had the energy to leave his apartment at all, since he must have known there was no reason to sit under a portapotty and watch the shit rain down on you. We met at the Alibi Room, found a corner, drank cheap beers, watching the other stiffs in suits drink their own cheap beers and flirt.

Scott brought five stacks of papers arrayed neatly in his messenger bag and handed them to me, and asked me to give them to Dundas, who was handling his classes on an emergency basis when no subs could be found. Trying to find a sub for Scott Sole is like trying to find a sub for Steve Jobs.

"You okay?" I said.

"I'm usually the one asking," he said. "I'm waiting for sentencing." He slid his hand along his neck.

"Why d'you say that?"

"I'm usually the guy who cleans up other people's messes instead of making them to be cleaned up. That's what this is about." He waved vaguely to the papers.

"Lesson plans?" I said. The top one mentioned how to traverse a doubly linked list in Python, which was a sibilant, hissing Greek to me but a computer language to the right people.

"You got it." He saw my puzzlement. "It's for my AP Computer Science class. The one where no one notices the work I do."

"*Plans*, with so little time left?"

"We get so little time with them, and then they're gone, out into the world. Depending on where they end up, some of them will vitally need to know comma rules and data structures if they're not going to get fired for incompetence."

"Scott, you need to lighten up. We should get another drink."

"And add public drunkenness? Nah. I already feel drunk. I need to see Kate. She'll take away my problems, just as she'll create them."

"That's hardly fair to her."

"You're right. Most of the time, your problems are your own creation. Why'd I choose such a stupid profession?"

"You're a teacher, not a rock star."

"Damn. Here I was, confused by all the groupies and paparazzi."

"Have you already been drinking?" I said. "I mean, before now?"

"Lola, baby—the. Milagro tequila, baby."

"Scott!"

"One sip never hurt anyone. I'd freshen up if Laura walked through that door and unbuttoned her blouse."

"There was that rumor about the Newport principal."

"Rumors. If we never trusted 'em, we'd be happier as a species."

"That's deeply philosophical."

"Yes, yes I am. Also, when I said Kate I meant Melissa. Kate and I, we're over."

"I'm sorry?"

"I'm not," Scott said. "By the way, how's the lucky guy from OKCupid?"

"Which one?" I said.

"The one who got lucky is the lucky one, obviously."

"Oh, him. He's good. Not at the introducing-to-friends stage, but getting there."

Scott didn't reply. I felt like I should check his pulse. I hated to see such a beautiful, beautiful man like this.

"So what next?" I said.

"I assume you get out of here before anyone sees you. You don't want to be seen with the leper, after all."

"Oh, Scott."

"Excuse me. The guy with the #EE2C2C letter."

"What?"

"#EE2C2C. It's hex for 'firebrick red.' "

"You are not wearing a scarlet letter."

"Metaphorically, we all are, when we treat anyone like she's wearing one. That's Hawthorne's point, at the end."

"Don't be ridiculous. I'm trying to help you."

"You are. It helps to talk it out. It's why I like novels—you get to talk it out with someone who's distilled years of thought into a convenient, two-to-twenty-hour package."

I assured him that I hadn't talked to the reporter, Lauren, who called and danced around her real purpose because, if she'd said it straight away, I'd have hung up. She might be nasty, but she knew her craft as well as anybody. Lauren started her interview with honey that concealed the final story's venom. By the time I told Scott as much, I wasn't sure he was still following the thought. Wasted, he was still cleverer than most people I knew, but he couldn't be bothered to appear to care.

• • •

Stacy Leon

Arianna called me one night. She said she wasn't going to talk to anyone about this ever again, but she had to admit what had happened, and when she got through it and the crying and the promises for me not to tell my parents, I was like, You are *such* a dumbass, Arianna, you could've written the stupid paper, gotten your C, moved on. That's what Mr. Sole would say. Why did I ever want you to like me? Why did I ever hang out with you?

Scott Sole

I wrongly felt like Winston in *1984*. Not that my predicament was comparable to being trapped in a totalitarian state. I needed a new job, which meant asking myself what I could do that others want to pay for. I could've tried to stay a public school teacher, but I didn't think I could face students and colleagues. It's hard to be a pariah, even for someone who imagines himself being prickily independent.

In those novels they never mention how much representation costs, if you get it. It's bad enough that the accusation ruins your life, practically burning it down. The drain on your wallet is like peeing on the ashes. Tom Killian sent me into debt, but I was ready to pay him whatever he wanted to keep me free.

• • •

Stacy Leon

I'm not the kind of girl who rats on her friends, but with Arianna lying to everyone, everywhere, I felt like I had to.

Most girls who say things like, "I'm not the kind of girl who…" is the kind of girl who…. does what she says she doesn't. Weird enough circumstances make us do weird things. Mr. Sole should know.

That's what I was thinking the day after the school year ended. Principal Shorewell was still at Herbert. Principals live in jail. I decided I wasn't going to make an appointment. I was going to march right in and tell her.

Except that when I opened the door to the administration's offices—it was weirdly heavy, like they didn't want me inside—Francine stared me down. It stopped me from going straight back.

"Can I help you?" she said.

"I'd like to—like to talk to Principal Shorewell."

"I'm sorry—she's in a meeting right now. However, the vice principal is available." Talking to him, the slob, about Arianna's sex life or lack of one grossed me out.

"I'll wait," I said.

"It might be a while."

"That's okay. It's really important."

I'd even remembered to bring a book. Scott always said that people with books are never bored, and when people said cell phone games are just as good, he'd say they were good for pretending not to be bored. I didn't know what to think. He also said there were some issues that you have to speak of, if you're going to be honest. Saying unpopular things means something. That's why he got in trouble.

One hour turned towards two while I read. *Blue Angel*—one of Scott's recommendations, and one I "borrowed" from my sister—seemed weirdly on point. The beginning scenes reminded me of our creative writing class, but I was really happy no one in my class wrote animal sex scenes.

Melvin Chang did write this one story about a poker playing vampire who leaves a casino, gets ambushed, murders like 12 people, and then has an orgasm. After, people were like, "You know, did you need a comma here?" and, "Your descriptions of poker are very real and detailed." Finally, Melanie Alexander was like, "I don't know about the orgasm thing," and everyone else was like, "Yeah, yeah, I agree." Now whenever I see him I can't help but think about that story. Maybe it isn't good to speak. Maybe I shouldn't. If you don't, the lies people believe spread, and other people get hurt, and silence contributes.

Before I could loosen my resolve and leave, Principal Shorewell appeared in front of me. She's unusually pretty. You wouldn't think that of a principal, but she was. Like a TV principal. She's the kind of person who would understand where I'm coming from if she wasn't *so* awkward.

Arianna Stephenson

In high school anytime you hook up the school knows on Monday. People whisper and text in the halls and caf. Guys watch like they think they're next. It's enough to make a girl not want to do it with anyone, ever, until she goes to college where no one knows or cares. My brother says people at UW take the walk of shame, but really it's a walk of triumph, because you got some. He sees girls doing it every weekend morning. And guys, too. He says the smart girls hold their heads up and give high fives to whoever—long as they're not too hungover. I wish I could be that kind of smart.

Everyone at school believed the story about me blackmailing Mr. Sole. Seriously. This counter-rumor swept the school, saying something kinda close to what really happened. Everyone was, like, against me, and stupid Sheldon would barely talk to me anymore. I'd never felt so alone. My parents said maybe I'd find a different school for my last year, and I was like, *Yessss*.

I can't wait for college. No more stupid *Scarlet Letter* paper. Ever again. Or scarlet letter. No scarlet Instagram. No more Mr. Sole. I hoped being in Europe that summer would help me forget him, and how he treated Sheldon and me when I just wanted to get in his stupid classes where he picks favorites. It's so *unfair*.

Scott Sole

Every story needs a villain. Stories without villains will have a villain inserted. In Lauren Reitman's article, I played Judas: betrayal of trust, shocking behavior, violation of fundamental values, disregard of taboo. She didn't put it in those terms, of course, because newspaper articles are written to flatter the ignorant prejudices of their readers, but that was her point. No one stops to ask, what values are being presented here? Could they be wrong? Could there be exceptions to underlying sets of assumptions?

No one takes the teacher's role. The artist's role. The novelist's role.

I wasn't yet overtly named, but anyone who knew Herbert would have to be daft not to know who the young, charismatic teacher with a strong online presence was. I hadn't thought about my resume since college. A quick search demonstrated: I still had the file.

• • •

Stacy Leon

I told her everything. She said she'd "look into the matter," and I started crying.

"What's wrong?" Principal Shorewell said. "You can tell me, honey."

I blubbered out that I was tired of Arianna's games, and what she was doing wasn't fair, I was so tired of her bullshit and ashamed to be her friend, or something like that.

"It's natural for you want to want to protect someone you care about," she said.

"What?" I said. I didn't want to protect Scott. I wanted to tell the truth.

"Nothing, honey," she said. "Have an almond and a tissue."

"Arianna," I said, "is a liar. She's always been a liar. I heard her telling Melanie Alexander and Quinn Hargreaves that the video thing last year was all my fault, and it's not true, it wasn't. It was all her idea. And—her—" I faltered.

"All your fault?" Principal Shorewell said. "Of course it wasn't."

"It wasn't! It was Sheldon's. He's the one who *made* us do it."

There was a big pause, like she didn't know what to do. Shit. I'd shifted to the video. But it seemed like Principal Shorewell was distracted or didn't care. She was looking into my eyes but like she was really staring fifty behind behind me.

"Honey, this is off the record, but you're almost an adult—no man can make you do anything. If he does, call the police. He can talk you into something you regret later, but to let him do that, you have to let him. If you're going to be a strong woman when you grow up, you have to understand that."

"I'm sorry. I didn't mean to say. It just—popped out."

"I understand."

"Are you going to, you know, do anything to him?"

"At this point, we'll see," Principal Shorewell said. She reminded me of my mom sometimes. Really cool, clinical. I didn't think the rumor about her and that guy from Newport was true. She didn't have it in her to break the rules.

"I didn't come in here to talk about that," I said. "I came in to say that Arianna, she made up the story about the sex with Mr. Sole because she didn't want to write her paper."

"I understand that you're frustrated," she said. "But what you believe about Arianna doesn't matter now, because we've begun a full investigation that will ascertain the truth of the matter."

She kept talking until I had nothing left to say, and I realized that I really needed to talk more to Melissa, not the principal. She'd know what to do. When I left Herbert for what I wished was forever, I also wanted to tell Mr. Sole so bad.

Then I started wondering: was she thinking that I wanted to protect Scott, or that I wanted to protect my sister? If I did, what from?

Arianna Stephenson

Principal Shorewell gave me an A for the semester, since I'd done pretty much all the rest of the work. I was so happy, and I'd worked so hard. I got to go to Barcelona. I filled out the Running Start application, and even though it was late, I got permission from the District to start at Seattle Central

Community College. Principal Shorewell helped me. She understood. Everything I'd ever wanted was coming true.

I feel sorry for Mr. Sole. I shouldn't've done what I did. But he also shouldn't've done what he did to me. We're even in a way. When what would've been my senior year started, I heard that practically everyone in school wanted to know what happened. Anyone who did know, like me and Melissa, wasn't telling. Only stupid Stacy did, to Principal Shorewell, and Stacy screwed up everything. Mr. Sole was okay. Not more. He kept updating his blog. Last I saw, he changed the logo to a red letter on a black background. Whatever.

When I came back from Europe, it was like I'd made a whole new life for myself, where no one knew who I was unless they looked me up on the Internet.

After all that happened, can you blame me for wanting to go to a party school? UW is filled with Asian nerds, cramming so they can be doctors, or whatever. I mean, I don't have a problem with Asian guys, and I've hooked up with one, but a whole school of people who study all the time is pretty lame, you know? I didn't think I'd get in, either.

I'm going to apply to Arizona and Arizona State. They practically don't have admission requirements. My parents said it would be a good idea for me to get out of the area and make new friends. They thought ASU and U of A would be too distracting, too much partying. But you know what? I love to party.

The girls in Arizona are so thin and pretty. Sometimes I don't think I'd fit in. Plus, the only people I know who want to go there have a really high BAC. It's better than a high GPA. That paper. I could've done better, but it doesn't really matter.

• • •

Scott Sole

My brief foray as a local celebrity had an unintended side effect that operated along the same principles that make serial murderers get marriage proposals. Mine was just a difference in scale. The first one came in an email from someone named "Elizabeth," no last name given:

"Heyyyyyyy i saw youre writing at work today when i was bored, we should hang ot you sound cool."

To its credit, the message ended with a period, and to the extent a woman's feelings about you can be gauged by the number of characters by which she extends a normal word, I was good. I wrote back a variation on something: "I'll definitely be hanging out with a girl tomorrow night—will it be you? Men are visual creatures. Send a pic or Facebook me."

An hour later Elizabeth chose Facebook chat, like they all do, and, based on her pictures, she wasn't bad; a bikini shot was in her first set. Bikini shots are basically the only reason straight men look through women's pictures, which women know though they may deny. And to see if she's got a rival. As far as I could tell, Elizabeth didn't, or didn't recently, but there were many, many pictures of her leaning into the chests of men with their arms around her. Based off her May birthday she was 20. Just. Like a few other Love Lab denizens I've met. How long will they live in the lab, as opposed to life? How long will I?

I was thinking about a reply, since she was definitely worth meeting, when I heard Ryan shamble in from work. If I'd been able to help the guy get a better job, I would have, but he seemed awfully close from my perspective to being a zero marginal product worker. Too many people without technical skills or inner drive are. Teaching taught me that not everyone can be taught, or helped.

I called out to Ryan. He opened the door to my room and probably saw me with that unnatural glow from the screen playing on my face like a reverse movie. We really are going to merge with the machines one day, but for now we use them to help us more effectively merge with each other.

"Check this," I said to Ryan.

He came behind me and read Elizabeth's message.

"Damn," he said. "She's okay. You don't know her or anything?"

"She found me out of the blue," I said. "Maybe that *Seattle Times* article."

"Women are crazy," he said. "Sending a loser like you a message. You have groupies."

"Or she's rational: she thinks I'm so desirable that a woman will cross every boundary to be with me. Transgression can be attractive. Why do you think certain drug dealers can get so much play, while your average programmer is jerking off to Internet porn?"

"Fuck, dude."

"Right. That's what I'm trying to do."

"Think she'll meet tonight?"

"I don't want to seem desperate, but why not? I said tomorrow. Maybe."

"Scott, I should also tell you something."

"Whether you have the clap is not important to me."

"This is important to you. And I'm sorry."

• • •

Laura Shorewell

Once the bureaucratic machinery starts, especially if the press is its impetus, it can't shut down instantly. What Stacy

Leon told me about Arianna was interesting, and something that I passed to district investigators, but we needed to do a thorough, complete examination of all allegations.

I saw more of Scott online, at *The Stranger* and elsewhere. Those pictures of women in bikinis might be old, but they can't be appropriate for a public figure charged with being a moral example to children. The man can't be teaching students with that kind of track record, no matter how often the students praise him.

It's a matter of protecting ourselves. I can't take one hysterical girl's word over another's. There are larger principles at stake here than girls ratting on each other, or ratting on boys, or gossiping about each other, or gossiping about boys. People have no idea the kind of stress I'm under, and the school has a reputation to protect.

Students might have a better experience if we weren't so focused on defense. But, however callous it might sound, sometimes a smooth ship requires someone to walk the plank for the good of everyone.

The whole Leon family is toxic.

Scott Sole

Elizabeth was the first stranger to contact me due to infamy but not the last. After Lauren Reitman's article was regurgitated because the visual vultures who feed off print got ahold of it, I was modestly famous in the northwest for all the wrong reasons. Said fame lasted about a week. My blog traffic spiked like I'd been caught in a celebrity sex scandal. Hundreds of people left comments reviling me. A guy with a little girl stared at me on 12th when I was walking through Capitol Hill. This in a neighborhood known for guys in drag and women frequently in fishnets and little skirts.

If women were a quarter as aggressive in real life with non-celebrities we'd live in a much happier, sexier, saner world. But they aren't, so you have to play or hack the game of the sexes as it is, unless you're a famous man. Normal guys line up for hot women.

If you want to be attractive to women, I can speak from experience that the only less popular topic to write about than books might be Unix or Windows systems programming. I didn't really choose what to write about; it chose me. An artistic outlet is done for the sake of art, not for the sake of women, regardless of what Freud and evolutionary psychologists say.

Stacy Leon

Sheldon found a new girl. He stopped returning texts. He wouldn't respond for hours, sometimes longer.

That left Arianna and me really on our own. There was a problem: I couldn't take Arianna without Sheldon as a buffer, and Arianna never forgave me for going to Principal Shorewell. There was Bill Wilson, too, but he circled like a moth attracted to light, not realizing how pathetic his crush really was. I liked him so much until he started to like me back.

When I realized what was happening, I hunted Sheldon down and demanded he say why he wouldn't hang out with us anymore. Something beyond that new girl. I *deserved* an explanation. I could say all the stuff he said and I said back, but it doesn't really matter: he never gave me one, after all I'd given him.

I told Melissa that I'd gone to Principal Shorewell. It was like she didn't even care. I thought she'd be angry, but she'd gone to that gray space past anger.

"It's because the district rescinded my contract," Melissa said. "I had it, then I didn't. Officially, budget cuts are the reason—Seattle has a last-hired-first-fired system. Unofficially, it's not that. It's everything else."

"What are you going to do for, like, a job?" I said.

"Not sure. Tutor. See if there are any desperate summer hires in the suburban schools. Schools can get around union hiring rules by posting summer emergency notices to replace teachers who wash out or whatever. That's how they can sometimes get young, fresh teachers and not the deadbeat ones who've been passed around too long in the dance of the lemons."

"Oh," I said, thinking about the dance of the lemons and what the hell she meant. "Why didn't you tell me?"

"I talked to Dundas a minute ago."

They'd planned it in advance. I wasn't the trigger. Melissa must've thought so. Otherwise she'd be pulling my hair and shouting, like she did when I stole her first bra and showed it to Mihaly Lavaris.

"Does that mean you're not going to move out?" I said.

"Don't sound so deflated. I'm exploring my options."

"Which are?"

"We'll see," Melissa said. "Besides, I need to move out, for my own well-being. And yours."

"I feel like I need to too. You got along with mom and dad so much better when you were in New York."

"In high school, I got tired of living in the future tense."

"I know exactly what you mean. I was thinking about it, and I might want to major in engineering. You know, build stuff. I always liked Mrs. Kissle's physics class, like with the catapults. I could see doing that."

"Why wait?"

"Yeah. I wonder what I should make."

"Repair bikes. Repair computers. Take stuff apart. I don't think it's that hard, not at first."

Melissa hugged me. Totally weird. She whispered, "No matter what, I still love you and you're still my sister."

She said, "You realize what you have to do, right?"

"No. What's that?"

"Call Lauren Reitman back."

"Why? D'you think she'll believe me?"

Melissa Leon

I'm a constant disappointment to my family. Almost as much as my oldest sister, the masseuse who really enjoys what she does—but my parents say things like, Try telling that to the Hildebrands at a cocktail party. Who cares what the Hildebrands think? They'd be impressed if I was a doctor, but have you *met* third-years and residents? The second most miserable people in the world, right behind the unemployed.

Before I'd really thought about what I was doing, I had made some quick flyers in Word and a barebones website from an online template. "Melissa's Quick Tutoring Company." Has a nice ring, don't you think?

• • •

Stacy Leon

Lauren didn't call me back right away. Maybe my message was too long. A day after I first called her, I called her again, and then Melissa suggested that I write an email. Does anyone write emails except for adults? I made an address and told her I had something to tell her.

She wrote back within half an hour to say that she'd been busy but would call soon. That day I stared at my phone, but the only texts I got were from Bill Wilson. He invited me to a movie and I accepted. It was time to do something normal.

Lauren called and as soon as I saw the funny number I knew it was her.

"Hey," she said. "What do you need to tell me?"

"Uh, hi," I said. "How are you?"

"Fine. What's up?"

"Arianna—she—I—I'm her best friend. She, like, told me, that, her paper, when it wasn't finished, she, um, thought that she didn't know what to do, about the paper, so she went to Mr. Sole's class after school—"

"What are you trying to say, Stacy?"

"That Arianna, she made up the story about Mr. Sole."

"How do you know?"

"She told me. She has reasons. It was a bad idea, I know, and she's very sorry now—"

"Why isn't she making this call?"

"She's too scared," I said.

"She needs to be the one calling me, and she needs to be the one talking to the police. You're the best friend, right?"

"I guess."

"So you shouldn't be doing this."

"I'm trying to stop Arianna from hurting anyone else. That's it. You're the person who can tell everyone the truth about what Arianna did."

Lauren sighed. I could tell she thought I was a silly, stupid girl who didn't know anything and was getting involved in matters that didn't concern me.

"I can't tell anyone anything that isn't true," Lauren said, "unless someone says it's true. I'm reporting the story, that's it. You need to go to the police, not talk to me, if you want to pitch this theory.

"Okay," I said. "But—"

"Or," she interrupted, "you need to get Arianna to make this call. Look, I've got to go. Anything else?"

I didn't say anything.

"Goodbye."

I texted Bill furiously about what had happened, and it was only a few hours later that I realized Lauren hadn't ever cared at all.

Scott Sole

The criminal case fell apart quickly, when the DA decided not to file charges because she lacked sufficient evidence, but the school's case dragged through months of interviews and discussions that boiled down to the classic he-said, she-said bullshit. None of the Herbert administrators contacted me. Stacy's testimony about Arianna's mental state and mendacity helped. But I had to produce all my grading records, which weren't in the ideal, pristine order they should've been in. Disorganization is not a crime. Yet. There was a great hole in them where Arianna's *Scarlet Letter* paper should've been, and smaller holes that various assignments should've occupied.

She was on the border of getting a C or D, and left to my own devices I would've given her a pity C in the hope that she'd wake up in college. Plenty of people do. But they claimed I'd given alcohol to minors, which wasn't true; I had occasionally seen former students at parties, where there'd obviously been booze, but it's not like I was busy reselling Bacardi handles behind the bleachers.

During summer I didn't have to show up to school. When the next year started, I realized that I wasn't going to get a class. I was being paid but reporting to the district office. It was mind-numbingly tedious. They had us doing database inputs and stamping letters. Sometimes I didn't do anything at all but sit in a cubicle, phones going off around me like fireworks, and read. Even if I was reinstated, so what? The better part of my life as a teacher was obviously done, and I wasn't the kind of person who worked for the weekends; I worked because my job was meaningful.

The only positive thing I can say is that I got started on another novel. The one about vampire hookers and faerie johns in nineteenth century London, using the supernatural creatures as an obvious metaphor for contemporary sexual problems, fell apart thanks to its bolted together and poorly defined feel, caused by my thinking about themes before story. Story is character and vice-versa. Characters are more than their libidos and job titles or you're writing porn or romance, which is porn for women. The characters were utterly dull. They had none of the sparkle of real-life people; none of them would've done what Arianna had done to me, although one, at least in my voluminous notes, was kind of like Arianna.

Instead I started writing about an inspirational teacher who discovers a magic lair that leads him and a handful of students into great danger and great possibility. Still speculative, but I knew a thing or two about the danger of knowledge, and I got halfway through before I realized I was really writing it. But I didn't get further than halfway, because the narrative petered out like a relationship with lots of sex and a declined invitation to the family's Thanksgiving. I couldn't go the artistic distance. The smartest thing any writer ever did was get out of the business.

Writing didn't get me my job back, though it did clarify what was real in my life and what wasn't. Being an artist wasn't. As the next school year started without me in front of a class, I realized the same thing I tell my students: if you're trying one thing, and it doesn't work, try something else.

Melissa Leon

Writing is so important to Scott that it became important to me. Most of my classmates in high school were oblivious: too much *Halo* addled the boys' brains. The girls cared about how much money their parents gave them to go shopping at the Seattle Center and the Northgate Mall, or whether their vibrator was charged (which, to be sure, is a universal concern). I thought everything would be better in college. It *is* better. Was better. But there were plenty of stupid rich kids at NYU, and now that I'm a little past that, I realize there're plenty of stupid rich kids everywhere.

But I was so furious that I began typing, thinking hotly the whole time of my time with Scott and how my horizontal education contributed to who I was much more than four years in undergrad. Or about the unfairness of the way people were talking about him, or how I could make my own decisions, no matter what bureaucrats thought about my sex life. It's counter-feminist, to take responsibility for your own actions. Before I knew what I was doing I had a couple thousand words. I wanted something confessional, something that started like this, with Scott's characteristic "So" that infects practically anyone who spends any time with him:

"So yes, I slept with my former teacher. My *former* teacher, after I was in his class. You know what? I'd do it again. That relationship was one of the most important of my life. The people writing about what happened don't know anything about me or about him, but that doesn't stop the horde of Internet idiots from spewing their bile at both of us."

All I cared about was the truth, no matter how stupid it was for me to care so much about this abstract thing. It doesn't even exist.

Lauren Reitman

Look, I don't really care who sleeps with who. But people always care about who does it with who. I follow the story, the story doesn't follow me. People like to read about the sex they wish they were having. If it were my daughter sleeping with her teacher, I'd do everything in my power to end him. What kind of parent would do otherwise?

I got a couple backdoor quotes from the girl's family's lawyer, who was authorized to leak and thus couldn't be trusted. If they had real evidence, the lawyer wasn't saying anything. Could mean they had real evidence, or it could mean they were fishing for a settlement. Either way, it made great news.

The day that story ran, the friend called to deny. I heard blah blah blah. Teenagers are unreliable. Talked about how she'd been the one who set things in motion by accident, how now this Arianna Stephenson was in over her head, and how the whole thing was a big misunderstanding. I was sitting in Cafe Zoka at the time, writing this little profile about a company named Delicious Monster, and tapping my pen—this wonder Pigma Micron 01 that gives great line—thinking, *Well, this story is good as dead if a quarter of her version's true.* Defending the teacher, what student *does* that? By then it was too late, and I let the stories stand, because you can't retract these things and hell, who'd trust an overly emotional teenage girl?

Scott Sole

Although I was never formally convicted—which is a phrase I never thought I'd write—the mob convicted me. My name became well-enough known to dominate the first page of Google results. My blog took first place for those "feeling lucky," but hits three to five described how terrible a person I, or the persona constructed by people who'd never met me, allegedly was. About accusations made, and descriptions—mostly false—of my many failures as a human being. I didn't read the details. Reading bad reviews is worthless. But I knew others would. Guilt by accusation has always been real. Even *The Stranger* covered me, cautiously and skeptically, implying the worst. Online culture is awful.

So I changed my name. It's the Internet-age online dodge for both victims and perpetrators. The process is easy for anyone without a criminal record. Nothing stops adults from changing our names. The instructions are like life itself now online. If I ever wanted another teaching job—or any job—I didn't have to worry about recommendations from Herbert. I needed to worry about what people would read on the Internet.

I began applying for teaching jobs. But the market had shifted under my feet, like a Mt. Rainer trail during a storm. A surplus of teachers were competing for jobs that had been cut during the deep recession and not restored after. A surplus of teachers accreted during my time at Herbert. Not even computer science credentials could get me over my own past. Good districts overflowed with candidates. Weirdly, principals friended me on Facebook. The second time that happened, I changed my Facebook name to a third choice. It was hard to keep my identities straight. It's like I wasn't the same person in all these places.

I wish there had been some catharsis there, but like most Americans I didn't and don't tolerate tragedy. I go for the laughs, the sex, the belief that the individual triumphs over his fate and time.

The name on my blog remained the "old" me, so prospective employers of the non-school variety would be able to find me. Sort of. In many mythic narratives, the rebirth of the hero is accompanied by a change in name and a growth of stature as the hero takes on adult responsibility and power over his people. In my case, it probably symbolized nothing; modern life is devoid of non-corporate symbols.

Denying the reality of change is a primary source of human suffering. I didn't find another teaching job, but years of teaching the equivalent of CS 101, 102, data structures, and algorithms made me employable in the tech industry. When I gave up on teaching, I found work for a growing company you've heard of, if you're young and cognizant. It hasn't gone public yet, but millions of people use its software every day, and although it has more than a thousand employees, it still has that startup feel.

It's so different from the classroom that I won't try to enumerate the ways. I find myself assuming my students' role—former students, that is—and struggling, successfully, to keep up with the work. The world is so big and school so small! There are small study groups around various subjects, like *The Art of Computer Programming*, or building your first compiler, or the Wizard book, or understanding Erlang. I go to many of them, maybe more than I should. I imagine myself leading them one day. For now, though, I'm struggling to keep and to find meaning.

I hadn't built any software systems with more than a thousand lines of code since I devised the computer science online testing system as a second-year teacher who wanted to automate as many tasks as I could. The pay is better but the hours are much, much longer. There isn't much non-technical teaching going on. As far as I knew, none of my coworkers developed crushes on me. I didn't have time to work on that novel anymore, because code consumed me. So did learning advanced topics that I'd neglected in my focus on beginnings.

Not long after I started, I was feeling lonely and didn't want to troll *The Stranger*, so I called Kate. She didn't pick up, but she did text me to ask what was going on, and I told her that I'd like to talk.

This time she did call. She listened to me talk about my life and laughed when I suggested we go out sometime, maybe to Canon, like the old days.

"Scott," she said. "I don't think that's a good idea."

"Why not?"

"I have a boyfriend now."

"A boyfriend? Why?"

"The same reason everyone gets a boyfriend."

"That sounds so unlike ... you."

"How would you know?"

She had a point.

I told her that if she wanted to see me, she knew where I was, but I didn't expect to hear from her again.

About a year into the new gig, I was working late when I saw a friend request: Melissa. I didn't know how she'd found me, given that I'd changed my name, but I did know how much I missed her. But I also didn't really want to accept her request.

I was momentarily paralyzed. To unfreeze myself, I opened a new window in my text editor. Telling my story seemed the simplest thing in the world and turned out anything but. There's still a great danger in donning a figurative scarlet letter, whether voluntarily or not. Mine would be voluntary. I had a platform. Maybe someone would care. I was probably wasting my time.

Still, I found myself smiling as I began to type.

###END###

Chapter 1 Romantic Dreams

I wanted to ask Anna to marry me, and I didn't. To resolve this problem, I decided that I couldn't entirely decide. But Anna was not the kind of woman who would wait indefinitely, and the end of our respective academic programs were in sight. She required commitment, and if she didn't get it she would let her work take her to the next stage of life leave me, like an expended fuel tank, falling back to earth. Her need of love and support would not impede her fundamentally goal-oriented dating philosophy.

At the same time these issues were becoming more and more salient, we were planning a trip to Seattle. I had to go, and Anna wanted to go, so I decided that I would decide by the end whether we should marry or split, with the intervening days devoted to seeking help from an unlikely source: old friends who would meet Anna for the first time. If you believe the pop psychologists, their first impression might be as good or better than the considered reactions of our friends in Tucson, who knew us both and were likely to render polite, judicious opinions based on knowing too much.

Travel reveals a person's character as no other activity can, and no person's character is as important as a romantic partner's. Consequently, there is no better test for a relationship than a trip, and ideally one to a location fraught with meaning for one or both parties, which will then reveal something of the past and present.

Journeys break down dignity and lower defenses. We cram ourselves into tiny metal tubes that hurtle through space at fantastic speeds in the hope that when we emerge on the other side, we will have changed places and allowed places to change us. Moving from our natural environment to a foreign one makes us confront the vicissitudes that disruption entails: the stoic breaks down in airport security, the daredevil declines to bungee jump, and the intrepid partier finds an early night unexpectedly more appealing than feeling up or being felt up by dubious human specimens at another club.

We have all seen travel companions behave differently than they do at home. When they are acquaintances, this might perturb us. When they are friends, our friendships deepen or fade under adverse circumstances like missed trains or departed planes or social diseases. But lovers might be the most revealing of all, because we share experience not only on a practical level but on a romantic level. If romantic decisions are among the most important we ever make, then we should search our partner's decisions for the personality facets they reveal: whether our partners want the French bistro or Chinese takeout, parks or theaters, tourist traps or townie dives.

With this in mind, I stood apprehensively in an improbably long security line at the Tucson airport, caressing a box in the pocket that contained my future while Anna caressed my other hand to dispel her nervousness. The truth about the nature of travel became more apparent when Anna abandoned my hand to root for her driver's license, muttering about potential mechanical malfunction, terrorism, and alien attack.

"It's in here somewhere," she said.

"You didn't leave it on the sofa," I said, "like that one time we went to Level and you didn't want to go, right?"

"You saw me take it."

"Yes—half an hour before we left. It could've slipped out since. Maybe you did it unconsciously because you don't want to go."

"I do want to go."

"But not on the plane?"

"It's illogical, I know, but please—no plane jokes."

"Not about hijacking, lightning, unladen swallows, drunk pilots—"

"Please!" Anna said, and took advantage of her right to throw herself into me. "I'm serious. Really, really serious."

"I'll try. I promise. But you're sure you didn't leave your license at home?"

"It's here. I'm positive."

"Did you check your rolly bag?"

"Right!"

She fished the main compartment and came up gold. Should *I* take charge of my own subconscious by slipping the ring box from my pocket, depositing it in one of the mailing envelopes that TSA offers to those with contraband, and sending it to myself. That, however, is a bit less subconscious than letting a license drop from a purse. Unlike Tolkien's Rings of Power, Rings of Marriage tend not to evade their owners' grasp unless willed to do so. My indecision was not so easily resolved by powers outside my control.

In taking Anna to Seattle, I hoped to find a sign, in an almost Biblical fashion, of whether I should proffer the ring. Modern life said it didn't matter much who I married: the wrong choice could be unmade by a lawyer in six months or six years. The financial cost might be high, but it would be bearable, and then I could assume the quest for the next woman. The cycle would repeat.

I still somehow felt the question of whether and who I married counted more than questions of my cultural reference points—*Harry Potter, The Name of the Rose, Seinfeld*—what car I drove—a Prius—or what computer I used—a MacBook Pro—no matter how those brand choices marked me as a man and a cliché. Aren't we more than the collections of things that we buy and the consumer preferences we have? Advertisers and marketers conspire to make us think the answer is "no," and I resisted them with the futility of a Japanese army detachment stranded after World War II. A vacation, however, might be a chance to get away from branding and towards a more authentic conception of the self, assuming that such a thing is possible.

The choice of a romantic partner carries greater symbolic than any other decision, for a failure in selecting a romantic partner feels like an essential failure of me as a person, rather than picking the wrong car or consumer electronic device, which are merely venal errors in momentary judgment that can be assuaged through liberal return policies or updated models.

My plan was almost discovered when a transport security woman asked to see my coat as it emerged from the scanner. She turned its pockets, emptying the ring box into one of those gray plastic bins suitable for remembering the Iron Curtain days as she searched for my keychain. Anna was still gathering her things, so I grabbed the box like a child snatching his toy.

"What's in there?" the woman asked.

"Nothing!" I said. "It's—for her—don't show her."

"I'll have to inspect it."

"It's a—take me in back. Please. Pretend I need a full cavity search."

She smiled, a willing conspirator among the normally stony bureaucrats, and led me to a small booth with a variety of stickers, instructions, and rules plastered about it. A man came in too, and he laughed when Rhonda—I saw her name tag—told him the reason as she opened the box and saw the ring.

"Is your girlfriend going to get it?" Rhonda said. "That's so romantic."

"No, it's for Hector, my Ecuadorian pool boy. Of course it's for Anna. I mean—it is romantic, but I'm not sure about giving it. I haven't decided. Yet."

"What're you waiting for? Christmas?"

To see her inner soul, to decide on whether we should embark on a life together, a signal from a God in whom I didn't much believe most of the time, except every other Rosh Hashana, when I sometimes engaged in a group religious ceremony with my parents, who also didn't much believe much. For some invisible line in my soul to be tripped, proving that Anna was unambiguously the right woman for me.

"I don't know," I said.

Anna had put her boots back on and looked erotically disheveled but nonetheless unhappy at having her dignity violated in the name of security theater.

"What was that about?" she said.

"Nothing," I said. "Routine. Random screening. Lucky my name isn't Mohammed, or I'd have been in there all day. Shipped off to Guantanamo Bay, never to be seen again."

"Random? You hiding secrets, Steven?"

"Not at all. I'm an open book."

"In that case, I look forward to your back pages and seeing how you end."

Anna is not a childish person—or so I had thought—but how well can we ever really know another? When I lived in Seattle, I took a special interest in *Seattle Times* stories about the men or women who leave for their proverbial pack of cigarettes and never return, the unexpected Craigslist killers, and the host of seemingly normal people who so defy expectations that we have trouble believing the idea of "normal." Yet we also cannot fully believe their loved ones' exclamations of shock and the claim that they lacked any warning. Perhaps if the family had gone from Seattle to London (or Tokyo or New York), the members would have discovered tendencies toward murder, abandonment, sadism, rape, or treating the nanny badly.

The issue of being childish or not arose in one of the obnoxiously loud airport bars. Anna drank half a beer and then insisted that I finish the rest because she planned to swallow Xanax and didn't want to accidentally end herself. Her need surprised me: Anna was confident in most situations, anxious in almost none, and mentally tethered with the ballast of classics—Dostoyevsky, Conrad, Austen—she'd consumed as a teenager, while I played video games and read endless science fiction. I thought she'd be typically sanguine. But airplanes were a weakness.

The plane departed fifteen minutes late. Anna fidgeted as I comforted, although my skill in that department has never been notable. The takeoff itself involved sweats on Anna's part, clutching my hand, a single tear, and tense waiting. Half an hour in, Anna pulled a small and much used stuffed giraffe from her purse. It was missing an eye.

"What's that?" I said, master of the obvious.

"My first friend. I don't generally show him to boys unless I have to. You should feel privileged."

"Plane flights only?"

"Yeah. Stephanopoulos normally sleeps under my bed."

"Near your vibrator?"

"No—what kind of sick man are you?"

"You, I believe, are the one who named your stuffed animal after a talking-head blowhard."

"Stephanopoulos was one of my first polysyllabic words. My parents watched a lot of political shows. It rubbed off."

"Enough to make you stay far from politics, it seems. I like that about you."

"And math."

"No wonder you're afraid of the flight: you don't know the math that dictates we'll stay in the air."

"Neither do you: for all you know, it could just be magical incantation."

"True. But I believe."

I also believed in Anna.

Or did I?

What else might Anna fear? And what would those fears say about her?

One former girlfriend, Sandra, hated camping in the Cascades, where she complained of the absence of structured activity and other people (though not in those words): she hadn't brought enough within her to appreciate the firs and pines, the streams that babbled like her friends, or the eastern gray squirrels chattering in the trees. Her suitcase contained her entire inner life, which I appreciated when I dragged its ineffective wheels up a staircase after we gave up on camping and went to a hotel with hot water and HBO on demand. She'd moved from Boston to Seattle with me and was, as far as I knew, still there, though not waiting for my return. I'd considered whether I should introduce Anna and decided against it. It's best to keep lovers separate unless you intend to love them together.

Another girlfriend, Stacy—do I gravitate toward sibilant names?—had an intense dislike of clowns that developed in childhood, as well as anxiety in groups of about six to twelve people, which she called an "awkward number," like the 800 meter in track: too small to be intimate but too large to lose yourself. She once leapt on the bed when she heard a noise that she feared was a mouse. To me, the only mice to be feared were those attached to a computer, which might cause carpal tunnel syndrome, and the noise Stacy heard was more like a piece of paper being torn than a mouse.

It turned out to be non-rechargeable batteries plugged into a charger. We broke up over other issues and cappuccinos at Stumptown, eyes as dry as the weather was not.

What did Anna's quirks say about her? Nothing, and everything. She has a peculiar way of cutting tomatoes. She is fond of dogs but finds cats haughty. She has surprising skill with a screwdriver and drill, which I say in a purely non-sexual context. She lifts her whole body slightly when she passes wind. These are all truths, but they come no closer to conveying who Anna is than the fetching crook of her nose, her superhuman ability to avoid stray hairs fluttering in front of her face, or her liking of bracelets. These inert facts somehow form the form of my love, and yet she is so much more than them.

"Would you like anything?" the stewardess asked.

Yes: to find the meaning of love through the slender window of our relationship and to know whether I should ask Anna.

"A tomato juice," I said.

"And you?"

"Vodka tonic, thanks," Anna said. If she wanted more love than vodka could provide, she kept that well hidden. I didn't inquire about her change of heart regarding alcohol and pills.

But I was ready to give her all the love I had, for I found being her protector charming, especially in a world where that role had been largely evacuated by professional police forces, felony convictions for fighting, antibiotics, condoms, feminism, airbags, and other social or scientific devices that one occasionally fantasizes about doing without before rolling over and grabbing the remote in order to watch *Terminator 2* or *The Incredibles*. I favor all those worthy things in the concrete (especially condoms), even when I imagine life, and my role in it, without them.

To have the talismanic powers of making Anna feel safe again made me feel, dare I say it, like more of a man—more of a man than reading *The Game* or anything else that describes being a man. Still, Anna's fear can be charming one moment but cloying or claustrophobic the next.

In that moment, however, I held Anna's hand all the tighter and passed my credit card, hoping that my gallant willingness to be charged $9 would be interpreted as it should.

http://www.amazon.com/Asking-Anna-Novel-Jake-Seliger/
dp/1495242218
The rest of Asking Anna is available at Amazon.com and through the iTunes Bookstore.

For more work by Jake Seliger, go to
http://jakeseliger.com.

Publishing a novel is hard for many reasons. One is finding people with skills many writers, including this one, lack. Here are some of the people who worked on Asking Anna:

Jenny Drewery copy-edited Asking Anna.
http://www.thewriterthebetter.co.uk/

Damonza designed the cover.
http://damonza.com/

Amy Siders, Corey Hodgson, and Robert Reid of 52Novels laid out the interior of the ebook and print book.
https://52novels.com

Julia Pinter made the author photo.
https://www.linkedin.com/profile/view?id=81299363